Waiting on GOD in a HIGH SPEED CULTURE

52 Devotions for Spiritual Growth in a Technology-Driven Society

RON CHIN

PRESS

TABLE OF CONTENTS

ACKNOWLEDGMENTS

Thank you to:

- Paul Chisaki and Tim Logan for reviewing the manuscript and providing great feedback.
- Jill Chin for reviewing and editing the manuscript.
- Dr. Lance Lee for providing encouragement during my seasons of waiting.

DEDICATION

To my wife, Jill
who supported me and grew with me
during a long period of waiting

INTRODUCTION

I f things had gone my way, I probably would not have written this book at this time. I would rather have been serving in a full-time ministry position. From 2012 to 2015, I had several solid job possibilities but in every case, something would occur and I would not end up getting a full-time offer. In one case, I was 99% sure that I was going to get a job after going through a four-month interview process. The organization told me that I was the only candidate for the job, and I had a great final interview with the person who would be my manager. However, a strange circumstance arose, and I did not get the position.

In 2015, I hoped that a part-time position would convert into a full-time position, but this did not happen and my wait continued. As a result of my circumstances, I gained a deeper insight into waiting on God and felt compelled to write this book. As I reflected on this topic, I realized that I repeatedly have gone through times of waiting on God since He called me out of my high-tech career into ministry in 2001. I have had periods of activity and productivity, but I also have experienced seasons of waiting in different areas of my life – while looking for a job, finding a wife, buying a house, and becoming a parent.

During this time when I have had prolonged periods of waiting on God, it seems that the pace of life in Silicon Valley and surrounding areas has become faster and faster. Adults and children work harder and harder to achieve more and more in this innovative, high-achieving area where I live. Patience seems to be a lost virtue and has been replaced by an increased need for instant gratification. This concerns me because waiting on God and having patience are important disciplines in developing a balanced and healthy lifestyle, which many people in Silicon Valley struggle to achieve. In this book, I consider the subject of waiting on God, with a particular interest in how it applies to the fast-paced, high-tech culture. Even if you are not involved with high-tech, I believe you will also benefit from this book.

Waiting on God may not seem to be an exciting topic, especially if you are an action-oriented person. However, as I have read the Bible, spent time in reflection and written about this subject, I have found that it is multifaceted and deeply interesting. Waiting on God can produce richness and depth in one's spiritual life. God uses waiting periods to deepen our faith, bring about spiritual maturity and prepare us for what lies ahead in our lives. As you read this book, I hope and pray that God will guide you into experiencing these benefits.

I have written 52 weekly devotions instead of daily devotions because after all, waiting on God can be a lengthy process. If you are going through a difficult season of waiting, you may find it helpful to read the devotions daily. Each devotion can be read in about five minutes and is followed by a short prayer. I recommend that you spend additional time reflecting and praying about the Scripture verses and material in each devotion. You may wish to keep a personal journal during your study to capture what God speaks to you and what thoughts and feelings come to you during different points in your journey of waiting on God. You may find that God is nudging you in a certain direction.

The devotions can also be used by groups in churches and in the workplace as a basis for a weekly discussion about waiting on God. The groups can give each member about five minutes to read a devotion and then proceed to have a discussion about the topic. Some of the devotions pertain to special days. Devotions for Easter, Pentecost, Thanksgiving and Christmas are designated in the Table of Contents. I pray that God will bless you and speak to you as you read this book.

DEVOTION 1
WHAT DOES IT MEAN TO WAIT ON GOD?

If you look up the meaning of the word "wait" in the dictionary, you will find multiple definitions:

- To stay in a place until an expected event happens, until someone arrives, until it is your turn to do something, etc.

- To not do something until something else happens.

- To remain in a state in which you expect or hope that something will happen soon.

If you try to come up with a definition of "wait on God" by looking at different passages in the Bible, you would also come up with multiple definitions because there are different aspects of waiting on God.

Nevertheless, I believe that there is one primary meaning of waiting on God in the Bible that applies to the life circumstances of many prominent Biblical characters—Abraham, Joseph, Moses, Hannah and David. Each of these people had to wait on God because they faced the following situation:

- God had a calling for them to do something in their life or

- God had promised them a blessing or they wanted a blessing from God or

- They found themselves in an unfavorable or undesirable situation

AND

- Nothing seemed to be happening or changing despite their best efforts.

If you face a situation like this today, then you will likely need to wait on God.

In his book *Waiting on God: Strength for Today and Hope for Tomorrow*, Charles Stanley provides this definition of waiting on God:

> Waiting on the Lord signifies an expectant endurance that is demonstrated by a directed, purposeful, active, and courageous attitude of prayer. [1]

In comparing this definition with the definition of "wait" provided above, notice that the main difference is that waiting is a passive activity, while waiting on God is a more active activity. Waiting on God requires the person to fervently engage God and to courageously persevere during a seemingly long period of time, believing that God will bring about what is best for the person's life. David had to go through a long period of difficult waiting in which his endurance and courage were tested. He wrote this:

> I remain confident of this:
> I will see the goodness of the Lord
> in the land of the living.
> Wait for the Lord;
> be strong and take heart
> and wait for the Lord.
> (Psalm 27:13-14)

Prayer

> God, give me the strength and courage to wait for you, no matter what circumstances that I currently face. Thank you that you are a good Father, and that you will bring about what is best for my life.

DEVOTION 2

FASTER IS NOT NECESSARILY BETTER

In 2013, I moved back to Fremont, California after having been away for nine years. Fremont is a city in the San Francisco Bay Area located between Oakland and San Jose. When I last lived in Fremont, it was a nice suburban town which had affordable housing. Upon my return, I noticed how much the city had changed during the past decade. The traffic was far worse, the housing was no longer affordable, the demographics had changed, and many of the schools had become very high-achieving and competitive. I concluded that a major reason for these changes was that, for better or for worse, Fremont had become part of Silicon Valley.

Psychologist Stephanie Brown has recently written a book called *Speed,* in which she concludes that many Silicon Valley people have become addicted to speed. She is not referring to a drug (methamphetamine); she is writing about a fast-paced lifestyle. In her book, Brown provides an insightful description of the culture of speed in Silicon Valley:

> While worry about speed is not a new idea, the current impact of speed on our culture is unprecedented and unforeseen. It is now causing serious damage to us as individuals and as a culture. The highest power economically, socially and within the family (as parents and schools push for kids to do more and more in order to "succeed") is now speed – moving constantly and moving fast. Fast means progress and success. Slow means failure. In the all-or-nothing American

culture, fast means you win and slow means you lose. It's as if we have moved from driving a highway at fifty-five miles per hour to sixty-five miles per hour to one hundred miles per hour; we can't slow down for the curves, and we are crashing. [2]

Silicon Valley has provided good jobs for thousands of people and birthed many useful advances in technology. However, there are downsides to this culture of speed and success:

- Stress – often there is so much work to do and the deadlines are short.

- Health – working long hours takes a toll on people's health.

- Family – Silicon Valley employees often are unable to spend as much time as they would like with their families.

- Spiritual life – often there is little time for a relationship with God and for serving God.

In the fast-moving Silicon Valley culture, people sometimes feel threatened by the competition and believe that they need to do more in order to keep up. In some cases, parents and children try to do more activities to make the children's qualifications for college look more attractive.

In the Old Testament, the kingdom of Judah struggled for survival due to the threat of the powerful nation of Assyria. Instead of turning to and trusting in God, Judah decided to take action and go to Egypt for help. The Prophet Isaiah spoke out against this action:

This is what the Sovereign Lord, the Holy One of Israel, says:

"In repentance and rest is your salvation,
in quietness and trust is your strength,

but you would have none of it.
You said, 'No, we will flee on horses.'
Therefore you will flee!
You said, 'We will ride off on swift horses.'
Therefore your pursuers will be swift!
A thousand will flee
at the threat of one;
at the threat of five
you will all flee away,
till you are left
like a flagstaff on a mountaintop,
like a banner on a hill."

Yet the Lord longs to be gracious to you;
therefore he will rise up to show you compassion.
For the Lord is a God of justice.
Blessed are all who wait for him!

People of Zion, who live in Jerusalem, you will weep no more.
How gracious he will be when you cry for help! As soon as he
hears, he will answer you. Although the Lord gives you the
bread of adversity and the water of affliction, your teachers
will be hidden no more; with your own eyes you will see
them. Whether you turn to the right or to the left, your ears
will hear a voice behind you, saying, "This is the way; walk
in it." (Isaiah 30:15-21)

Instead of rushing off to find a human solution to the problem,
the people were encouraged to turn to God, be quiet and rest. When
people feel threatened and believe that they need to take quick action,
they often find it difficult to think clearly and to hear God's voice.

In our high-tech culture, this is an important truth to take hold of. If we can slow down, rest and seek God, we will be better able to discern God's leading and hear his voice saying, "This is the way; walk in it." When we are in tune with God and his plan for our lives, then we can have a quiet confidence in the path which we are to follow.

Prayer

God, in the midst of this fast-paced culture, I recognize that I have a choice about my lifestyle. I choose to have a lifestyle of repentance and rest, and of quietness and trust in you. I desire not to be driven by my fears. Help me to slow down and to hear your voice, so that I can walk in peace in the direction that you want me to go. Thank you for your graciousness and compassion.

DEVOTION 3
GOD HAS A PLAN FOR YOUR LIFE

Waiting is difficult. Nobody likes to wait for something that is unlikely to happen soon. It is easier to wait when you believe and trust that God has a plan for your life. A popular Bible verse about God's plans for people's lives is Jeremiah 29:11: "For I know the plans I have for you," declares the Lord, "plans to prosper you and not to harm you, plans to give you hope and a future." This verse brings great encouragement to many people who struggle with their present circumstances. However, people who hold onto this promise may lack an understanding of the characteristics of God's plans. By reading the verses surrounding Jeremiah 29:11 and examining the context of this passage, we can get a deeper understanding about God's plans for people's lives.

Jeremiah, one of God's prophets in the Old Testament, wrote to the Israelites who lived in exile in Babylon, away from their cherished Promised Land:

Yes, this is what the Lord Almighty, the God of Israel, says: "Do not let the prophets and diviners among you deceive you. Do not listen to the dreams you encourage them to have. They are prophesying lies to you in my name. I have not sent them," declares the Lord." This is what the Lord says: "When seventy years are completed for Babylon, I will come to you and fulfill my good promise to bring you back to this place. For I know the plans I have for you," declares the Lord, "plans to prosper you and not to harm you, plans to give you hope and a future. Then you will call on me and come and pray to me, and I will listen to you. You will seek me and find me when you seek me with all your heart." "I will be found by you," declares the Lord, "and will bring you back from captivity. I will gather you from all the nations and places where I have banished you," declares the Lord, "and will bring you back to the place from which I carried you into exile." (Jeremiah 29:8-14)

Here are some important things we can learn about God's plans from this passage:

God loves us and has a good plan for us despite our failings

For many years, the Israelites did not serve God with their whole hearts. They did not listen to God and worshipped the idols of the neighboring countries. Although the Israelites had turned away from God, God still loved them and did not abandon them. He had a good plan for them in the future.

God's plans are good, but they may not sound good to us initially

When the Israelites went into exile to Babylon, they understandably felt very discouraged. In this state of mind, they probably would have been yearning to hear something positive from God. A false prophet, Hananiah, had said that they would return from exile within two years. Although this message sounded good, it did not correctly state God's plan. Jeremiah clearly told the exiles that God had a good plan for them, but it would take 70 years for God to fulfill the plan. This news probably was a bitter pill for the exiles to swallow. However, during the 70 years, God used Daniel, one of the exiled Israelites, in a profound way to show God's power to the Babylonians. Eventually, the Babylonian empire fell to Medo-Persia and King Cyrus, who allowed the Israelites to return to their country.

God's plans are not on our time table.

The exiles would have to live in Babylon for a really long time—70 years. Certainly, God's timeframe for their return to Israel seemed very long to them. As I write this, I have been without a full time job for almost three and a half years. While this period of time has lasted much longer than I desired, God has provided for my wife and me, and I continue to wait on God.

God's plans often involve restoration, redemption and reconciliation.

God's plans for the people who lived in exile in Babylon reflect some major themes of the Bible—redemption, restoration and reconciliation. God sent his son Jesus in order to redeem humanity from Satan and sin, and to reconcile humanity to God, so that we can be restored into a loving relationship with him.

Prayer

God, I thank you that you desire to bring redemption, reconciliation and restoration to people. I thank you that you desire to give me a future and a hope. Help me to embrace your plans for my life, even though I may not initially like the plans and their time table.

DEVOTION 4
GOD WORKS IN MYSTERIOUS WAYS

In 2001, Bill, a retired pastor from the United Kingdom, came to stay at my house. When he spoke at our church, he talked about his mission trips to Malawi, a country in Africa. As he spoke about his great experiences there, I thought to myself, "It would be kind of cool to go on a mission trip there." When I went to work the following week, I found it strange that I could not login to my computer. A few minutes later, my manager contacted me and asked to meet with me. I went to her cubicle and she told me that the company was having a layoff and I had lost my job. I was kind of shocked! I had only worked at this start-up company for about three months. I had never been laid off before or gone through unemployment.

After I got over the shock of losing my job, I thought about going on a mission trip with Bill. He told me that he had another trip to Malawi planned in about three months. I began to pray seriously about going on the mission trip. Because I have never been an adventurous type of person, I had some fears about going to a poor, third-world country that had serious problems with AIDS and malaria.

After I spent time praying and thinking about the mission trip to Malawi, I felt that God wanted me to go. I went to my doctor's office, received multiple shots in both arms, and got a prescription for anti-Malaria medication. I also bought a mosquito net and some emergency food rations. In August, 2001, I boarded a plane for the UK to join Bill and his team. We spent about three weeks in Africa with a pastor in Malawi named Booker. What an incredible three

25

weeks we had! Malawi has been nicknamed the Warm Heart of Africa, and I found this to be true. The people in Malawi were wonderful and friendly. Most people didn't have much money or food, and many people were ill with malaria or AIDS. However, the people there seemed happy.

The mission trip had a tremendous impact on my faith. I had to let go, allow God to be in control, and depend on God. As I did this, I saw what God can do. He orchestrated an incredible three weeks in Africa. I experienced God moving more powerfully than I ever had before. I have heard other Christians express similar sentiments when they went to third world countries to minister. In the US, because we live in a generally affluent society with good medical care and education, we don't have to rely on God so much. On the other hand, the people in third world countries usually don't have money in the bank, good health care or good education. Therefore, they have to trust in God and have faith in God. In this environment of faith, God seems to move more powerfully.

My experience in Malawi was so different than my normal life in the US. Sometimes, we went shopping in Malawi and bought rice for dinner. We found out that most people in Malawi could not afford to eat rice, the staple of many Asians' diet. The people in Malawi didn't have much in terms of material things, and things did not get done efficiently because the pace of life was much slower. However, the people in Malawi were very friendly and seemed to be happy. I had gone on the mission trip to help the people in Africa, yet I found that I actually needed to learn something from them. I realized that I had some problems in my life. I was too driven to succeed and focused too much on doing things efficiently. I found my time in Africa to be healing for me and that I actually received more than I gave.

My experiences also reminded me that we live in a broken world. In the US, we can have kind of a sheltered life, not seeing the brokenness of people and their need for God. I could no longer work at a well-paying job that didn't have much meaning for me. God was calling me to make a difference in a broken world. Shortly after I returned from the trip, I felt convinced that God wanted me to leave my career in high-tech and serve him in ministry. I had one of the best experiences of my life on that mission trip. Losing my job turned out to be a tremendous blessing to me. The apostle Paul wrote:

> And we know that in all things God works for the good of those who love him, who have been called according to his purpose. (Romans 8:28)

Prayer

> God, I believe that you are working for my good, even when circumstances don't look favorable. Help me not to get discouraged, but instead to wait to see the blessings that you have for me as I follow you.

DEVOTION 5

THE DANGER OF COMING UP WITH A HUMAN SOLUTION

Abraham and Sarah (named Abram and Sarai before God gave them new names) waited for a decade for God to deliver on his promise of a child, but nothing seemed to be happening. Then Sarai came up with an idea:

> Now Sarai, Abram's wife, had borne him no children. But she had an Egyptian slave named Hagar; so she said to Abram, "The Lord has kept me from having children. Go, sleep with my slave; perhaps I can build a family through her."
>
> Abram agreed to what Sarai said. So after Abram had been living in Canaan ten years, Sarai his wife took her Egyptian slave Hagar and gave her to her husband to be his wife. He slept with Hagar, and she conceived.
>
> When she knew she was pregnant, she began to despise her mistress. Then Sarai said to Abram, "You are responsible for the wrong I am suffering. I put my slave in your arms, and now that she knows she is pregnant, she despises me. May the Lord judge between you and me." (Genesis 16:1-5)

Sarai's statement, "The Lord has kept me from having children," was accurate. The Lord was in control of this matter. Perhaps after ten years, it seemed to Sarai that God would never allow her to have children. Therefore, she came up with a solution that was common in their culture and proposed it to Abram. We do not know what went through Abram's mind as he considered this solution. Perhaps he thought that Sarai's plan did not explicitly go against God's promise to Abram—"a son who is your own flesh and blood will be your heir" (Genesis 15:4). However, it appears that Abram did not consult God before deciding to go ahead with Sarai's plan.

Sarai's solution caused troubles from the beginning. Sarai's slave, Hagar, developed a bad attitude after she became pregnant and had a conflict with Sarai. After Hagar ran away from Sarai, an angel of God told Hagar that her son, Ishmael "will be a wild donkey of a man; his hand will be against everyone and everyone's hand against him, and he will live in hostility toward all his brothers" (Genesis16:12). Charles Stanley, in his book *Waiting on God*, writes about Ishmael's descendants, who settled in the territories east of Israel:

His descendants, the Ishmaelites, intermarried with the nations inhabiting this vast territory – from the Suez Canal through Sinai and north across the Saudi Peninsula to what is modern-day Iraq – and they became the Arab peoples who have been a constant source of conflict for Israel. ... think about how vastly different and undoubt- edly more peaceful Israel's existence would be if Abraham and Sarah had simply waited on God and had not contrived their own way of making the promise come true. To this day, their descendants are suffering the consequences of their actions. [3]

Although Abram and Sarai made a mistake which caused many future problems, God showed mercy and grace, and did not change his promise to them. 14 years later, God fulfilled his promise when Abraham and Sarah became the parents of Isaac.

In our modern, well-educated society, it may seem perfectly nat- ural to come up with human solutions to problems. Silicon Valley has a lot of smart people who commonly use their brain power to innovate and solve complex technical challenges. The Internet has made so much information and knowledge available to help people make educated decisions. However, we have to take caution when coming up with our own solutions because God says, "As the heavens are higher than the earth, so are my ways higher than your ways and my thoughts than your thoughts" (Isaiah 55:9). A possible solution to a problem may initially look good, and it may seem prudent to go for it. Even godly people like Abram sometimes plow ahead without prayer. God has given each of us a brain to use. However, it is wise to involve God in decision making and consult him before moving forward. This can save us from having a lot of heartache.

Prayer

God, forgive me when I have come up with my own solutions and moved forward without consulting you. Thank you for your forgiveness and grace. I desire to hear your voice, so that I can know your wisdom and guidance for my situation.

DEVOTION 6
WAIT IN FAITH OR STEP OUT IN FAITH?

A life of faith requires two different types of responses to God – waiting in faith and stepping out in faith. Abraham, known as the father of faith, responded to God in these two distinct ways during different seasons of his life. After Abraham's father died, God called Abraham to leave his father's household and to go to a new place. Abraham stepped out in faith and travelled to the land of Canaan. The author of the book of Hebrews wrote, "By faith Abraham, when called to go to a place he would later receive as his inheritance, obeyed and went, even though he did not know where he was going." (Hebrews 11:8)

Abraham and his wife Sarah prospered and settled in the land of Canaan. However, they had some feelings of despair because they did not have any children. Then, one day, God spoke to Abraham and promised that he would have a son. Abraham believed God and began to wait. Abraham had to wait...and wait... and wait. Finally, when his wife Sarah was past the age of childbearing, God miraculously allowed them to become the parents of Isaac. Abraham waited for about 24 years. That's a long wait!

At certain points in your life, you may face difficult decisions in regards to a new possibility or direction. These decisions often require discernment about whether to step out in faith or to wait patiently in faith. Perhaps you face one of the following decisions:

- You want to purchase a home in an area with increasingly expensive housing. Should you purchase a house, rent and wait, or move to another area with more affordable housing?

- You have a job opportunity with a start-up company. Should you go to the start-up or stay with your current job, which is more stable?

- You have a good job but don't really like what you do. Should you stay with your job or make a career change?

- You and your spouse want to become parents, but are having difficulties conceiving. Should you try in-vitro fertilization (IVF), adopt, or continue to try to have a child the conventional way?

The key to making a good decision in these matters is keeping in step with the Holy Spirit:

But the fruit of the Spirit is love, joy, peace, forbearance, kindness, goodness, faithfulness, gentleness and self-control. Against such things there is no law. Those who belong to Christ Jesus have crucified the flesh with its passions and desires. Since we live by the Spirit, let us keep in step with the Spirit. Let us not become conceited, provoking and envying each other. (Galatians 5:22-26)

In this letter to the Galatian church, Paul encouraged the believers not to live by the selfish human nature, which he also called "the flesh." Then, he used military language ("keep in step") to describe how the believers should respond to the Holy Spirit.

Paul knew that there are some different forces that can cause a person to get out of step with God. In the honor and shame-based Mediterranean culture in which Paul lived, people often competed for honor and envied each other. This was one outcome of people living by their flesh. I believe that Paul wanted to communicate this to the Galatians: "Let's not get caught up in competition, envy, and trying to be better than others. Let's not get off track. Instead, let's keep in step with the Spirit."

In the high-tech culture, the competition is fierce and technology changes rapidly. Therefore, people tend to take action rather than to wait. However, God might call us to wait even though it may not make sense in this fast-paced culture. I think that God would say, "Don't keep in step with the high-tech lifestyle; keep in step with the Spirit." Sometimes the Spirit will lead us to wait and have patience. At other times, the Spirit will lead us to step out in faith. If the Spirit says, "Wait," we should wait. If the Spirit says, "Go," then we should go.

Prayer

God, help me to be sensitive to the movement of the Holy Spirit in my life and in the lives of the people with whom I interact. Give me the wisdom and discernment to know when to step out in faith and when to wait in faith. Help me to trust you and to have courage whether you call me to step out in faith or wait in faith.

DEVOTION 7
WAITING AND PERSONALITY — PART 1

When I became a pastor, I found that one of the challenges was shepherding a group of people with many different personalities. In order to help each person grow, I had to understand what made each one tick. Also, I had to take into account what one of my former pastors taught me: "God treats us individually." This means that the way God shapes a person to become spiritually mature differs somewhat from individual to individual.

In the previous devotion "Wait in Faith or Step Out in Faith?," we considered that the Christian faith requires two different responses to God. An individual's personality will often have a strong influence on which of these two responses a person has difficulty with. For example, in the Bible, Peter had an impulsive, bold personality and was quick to say what he thought. In the Gospel accounts, Peter showed a proclivity to jump into things and not to wait in faith:

- Peter tried to walk on water with Jesus but failed because of his lack of faith.

- When Jesus told his disciples about his upcoming suffering, death and resurrection, Peter thought that this was horribly wrong and began to rebuke Jesus.

- After proclaiming that he would lay down his life for Jesus, Peter denied Jesus three times.

Despite Peter's shortcomings, Jesus did not give up on him. He continued to love him and shape him into the person that God created and wanted him to be. After Jesus' resurrection, he taught Peter and some other disciples through a meaningful appearance:

> Afterward Jesus appeared again to his disciples, by the Sea of Galilee. It happened this way: Simon Peter, Thomas (also known as Didymus), Nathanael from Cana in Galilee, the sons of Zebedee, and two other disciples were together. "I'm going out to fish," Simon Peter told them, and they said, "We'll go with you." So they went out and got into the boat, but that night they caught nothing.
>
> Early in the morning, Jesus stood on the shore, but the disciples did not realize that it was Jesus. He called out to them, "Friends, haven't you any fish?" "No," they answered. He said, "Throw your net on the right side of the boat and you will find some." When they did, they were unable to haul the net in because of the large number of fish. Then the disciple whom Jesus loved said to Peter, "It is the Lord!" As soon as Simon Peter heard him say, "It is the Lord," he wrapped his outer garment around him (for he had taken it off) and jumped into the water. (John 21:1-7)

When Peter had this experience, he surely had a flashback to the events chronicled in Luke 5, when Peter decided to follow Jesus after Jesus helped him to catch a great number of fish after a night of unfruitful fishing. Jesus was teaching him the same lesson again! Jesus showed Peter, who made his living as a fisherman, that he could not do things out of his own wisdom and strength, and that he needed to wait on and rely on God. A modern day example is a programmer who stays up all night trying to make a computer system work. The programmer fails, but then Jesus shows up and makes the system work.

After Peter realized it was Jesus, he displayed his impulsive personality – he jumped right into the water. However, this act was not like one of the unwise actions he had taken previously. Peter's desire was to get to the shore to greet and be with Jesus. That was a great place to be!

In the book of Acts, we see a changed Peter. He continued to have boldness, but it was a God-shaped boldness. He spoke wisely and convincingly on the day of Pentecost, when three thousand people became followers of Christ. He endured being persecuted and incarcerated by King Herod, and walked out of jail when God miraculously freed him. When Peter wrote a letter to believers (1 Peter), he encouraged them to rejoice in God and persevere in times of trials and suffering. This encouragement came from a person who had learned to wait on the Lord.

Prayer

God, forgive me when I act impulsively and don't consult you before I speak or take action. Thank you for your great forgiveness. Help me to walk in humility and to have a God-shaped boldness.

DEVOTION 8
WAITING AND PERSONALITY – PART 2

The apostle Paul wrote the following words of encouragement to Timothy, a young man who he mentored:

Don't let anyone look down on you because you are young, but set an example for the believers in speech, in conduct, in love, in faith and in purity. Until I come, devote yourself to the public reading of Scripture, to preaching and to teaching. Do not neglect your gift, which was given you through prophecy when the body of elders laid their hands on you. (1 Timothy 4:12-14)

I am reminded of your sincere faith, which first lived in your grandmother Lois and in your mother Eunice and, I am persuaded, now lives in you also. For this reason I remind you to fan into flame the gift of God, which is in you through the laying on of my hands. For the Spirit God gave us does not make us timid, but gives us power, love and self-discipline. (2 Timothy 1:5-7)

Based on statements like these in Paul's letters, some people infer that Timothy was a timid person. However, the Bible does not provide any concrete proof of this. Actually, Paul respected Timothy greatly and wrote, "...Timothy has proved himself, because as a son with his father he has served with me in the work of the gospel" (Phil 2:22). Paul chose Timothy, a young man, to go on a very difficult assignment—to lead the Ephesian church, which had some older people. Therefore, perhaps the best way to view Timothy is as a faithful, young leader who had a less forceful personality than others in leadership.

Paul's exhortations to Timothy provide useful guidance to people who have a less forceful personality. Those who are less bold typically feel more comfortable waiting in faith than stepping out in faith. Paul exhorted Timothy to take action by telling him:

- You have a sincere faith. Paul felt comfortable with Timothy exercising his gifts in a leadership role because of his good character and faith. Good character is a requirement for leadership; a forceful, upfront personality is not.

- God has given you spiritual gifts to use. People may look at their own characteristics – their age, marital status or public speaking ability – and feel intimidated. In my first pastoral position, I was a single man ministering to a congregation with many married people, some of whom had children. However, I came to realize that God had equipped me with certain gifts to minister to the congregation.

- Church leaders have laid hands on you. Both the apostle Paul and the elders of the Ephesian church had recognized God's calling for Timothy and imparted him with spiritual gifts. Timothy did not operate independently. He had a mentor (Paul) and a group of elders with whom he co-labored. When stepping out in faith, it is helpful to have relationships with leaders who can provide encouragement, wisdom and accountability.

It is important for a person to neither walk ahead of God nor walk behind God. If a less forceful person tends to wait in faith rather than step out in faith, they may find that God is waiting for them. If this is the case, then it is a good idea not to keep God waiting. As one of my friends says, "Don't say no when God says go!"

Prayer

> God, I pray that I will not walk ahead of you and that I will not walk behind you. Help me to step out in faith when you call me. Help me to rely on you and the gifts that you have given me.

DEVOTION 9
WAITING SHOWS US WHO'S IN CONTROL

Many people in foreign countries live under the control of oppressive leaders or political systems that limit their freedoms and opportunities. Despite its problems, America remains an attractive destination for immigration for many people. America offers the opportunity for "life, liberty and the pursuit of happiness." This is especially true for Silicon Valley, as large number of immigrants have flocked to the area for the opportunity to prosper economically.

The Bible contains a famous story about God's people escaping from oppression and moving to a land of prosperity. At the beginning of the book of Exodus, the Israelites lived as slaves under the control of the Egyptians, who mistreated them. God miraculously parted the Red Sea and allowed them to escape from the Egyptians. God showed them his power and that he was in control of their future. God wanted to bring the Israelites into the Promised Land, a place with plentiful agricultural resources. However, when God told them to enter, they feared the people who lived there instead of believing that God was in control. The Israelites did not trust God and rebelled. It was possible that they carried some wounds from having been mistreated and controlled by the Egyptians.

As a result, the Israelites wandered in the desert for 40 years, waiting for God to give them another opportunity to enter the Promised Land. During this period of time, God molded and shaped the people. After 40 years, as the Israelites prepared to enter the Promised Land, Moses spoke these words to them:

When you have eaten and are satisfied, praise the Lord your God for the good land he has given you. Be careful that you do not forget the Lord your God, failing to observe his commands, his laws and his decrees that I am giving you this day. Otherwise, when you eat and are satisfied, when you build fine houses and settle down, and when your herds and flocks grow large and your silver and gold increase and all you have is multiplied, then your heart will become proud and you will forget the Lord your God, who brought you out of Egypt, out of the land of slavery. He led you through the vast and dreadful wilderness, that thirsty and waterless land, with its venomous snakes and scorpions. He brought you water out of hard rock. He gave you manna to eat in the wilderness, something your ancestors had never known, to humble and test you so that in the end it might go well with you. You may say to yourself, "My power and the strength of my hands have produced this wealth for me." But remember the Lord your God, for it is he who gives you the ability to produce wealth, and so confirms his covenant, which he swore to your ancestors, as it is today. (Deuteronomy 8:10-18)

Moses told the people that the 40 years of wandering and waiting in the desert had a purpose. The desert was a dangerous place with little water and food, and the Israelites were not in control of their own survival. God humbled them and forced them to rely on him. God tested them to see if they trusted him and believed that he was in control. God desired that when the Israelites settled and prospered in the Promised Land, they would not become proud and self-sufficient, forgetting that he was the one who was in control.

In the world of high-tech, it is easy to believe that being smart, innovative, technologically savvy, hard-working and quick-thinking

41

produces personal wealth. Therefore, many people charge ahead and try to develop these qualities. Many people succeed, but at the same time, pride may begin to grow, which in the long term causes problems.

It is important to remember that our lives, minds, strength, gifts, abilities and talents come from God. Waiting is one of the tools that God uses to show us who is in control. When we face a situation in our lives in which we have to wait, it is difficult because we don't have control of the situation. During a period of waiting, we may feel like we're wandering in the desert. You may be waiting for a job, struggling with a long time illness, or hoping for a spouse or a baby, and you don't see the end in sight. God wants to teach us that ultimately, we are not in control. If you are struggling during a time of waiting, consider that the wait could be a blessing in disguise. You can grow in your knowledge that God is in control, so that "in the end it might go well with you."

Prayer

> While I am waiting on you, God, teach me humility and reliance on you. I recognize that all of my gifts, abilities and talents come from you, and that ultimately, I am not in control. Thank you God that you are in control and that the lessons you are teaching me are for my benefit.

DEVOTION 10
LEARNING TO BE A SERVANT

After God had called me to go into ministry, I decided that I would leave high-tech and look for a ministry position. I found a church position that appeared to be a good fit and went through the initial stages of the interview process. The church felt that I was a good candidate for the position and paid for me to take an airplane flight to visit them and to have a face-to-face interview. The visit went well and I expected to get an offer from the church. To my surprise, the church notified me that they had taken another look at their finances and decided that they could not hire me. As a result, I had to wait to start my new career. God had something else in mind for me.

At this time, I owned a house and I needed some income to pay for the mortgage and my living expenses. A friend contacted me and told me that his employer, a start-up high tech company, had a temporary job opening. I went for an interview and found out that the job paid less than half of what I had earned before. However, the salary basically covered all of my expenses, so I decided to take the position, which involved working primarily as a shipping and receiving clerk. I packed and moved a lot of boxes, and became proficient at using a hand truck and a tape gun. There was nothing wrong with the kind of work I did. It was a good honest work. However, it was a humbling experience for me because I worked at a job that was far below my capabilities. During this period of time, I began to realize that this was part of God's preparation for me for ministry. God wanted me to gain a deeper understanding about servanthood.

Jesus' disciples had to learn a similar lesson as they spent time with Jesus. One day, the mother of two of His disciples, James and John, went to Jesus to try to obtain positions of honor for her two sons. This caused a big argument among Jesus' disciples, and Jesus had to break up the conflict:

> Jesus called them together and said, "You know that the rulers of the Gentiles lord it over them, and their high officials exercise authority over them. Not so with you. Instead, whoever wants to become great among you must be your servant, and whoever wants to be first must be your slave— just as the Son of Man did not come to be served, but to serve, and to give his life as a ransom for many." (Matthew 20:25-28)

In their culture, there actually were servants and slaves who made up the lower echelon of society. The average person cared about maintaining their honor and social status, and definitely wanted to avoid becoming a servant or slave. However, Jesus told his disciples that to be great in his kingdom, they would have to be like servants and slaves. Jesus didn't want his disciples to be concerned about their own honor or status. Instead, he wanted his disciples, who would become the leaders of the early Christian church, to serve people rather than to lord their position of power and status over others.

It is easy to be lured into thinking that greatness resides in people who have the most talent, the most money, the highest job title or the most social media followers. The truth is that the measure of true greatness has to do with servanthood, which Jesus modeled for us. Servanthood starts with receiving Jesus' great service to us. Jesus, who was God in the flesh, set aside his status and became a servant who paid the price for our freedom from the power of sin and shame. That was an incredible picture of servanthood!

Prayer

> Jesus, I thank you that you humbled yourself and came to this earth to serve all of humanity. Whatever position you place me in, help me to have the attitude of a servant. I choose to serve others as you have served me.

DEVOTION 11

DOES TECHNOLOGY SERVE US OR DO WE SERVE TECHNOLOGY?

After the Israelites had entered the Promised Land, Joshua spoke these parting words to the people before he died:

> "Now fear the Lord and serve him with all faithfulness. Throw away the gods your ancestors worshiped beyond the Euphrates River and in Egypt, and serve the Lord. But if serving the Lord seems undesirable to you, then choose for yourselves this day whom you will serve, whether the gods your ancestors served beyond the Euphrates, or the gods of the Amorites, in whose land you are living. But as for me and my household, we will serve the Lord."

> Then the people answered, "Far be it from us to forsake the Lord to serve other gods! It was the Lord our God himself who brought us and our parents up out of Egypt, from that land of slavery, and performed those great signs before our eyes. He protected us on our entire journey and among all the nations through which we traveled. And the Lord drove out before us all the nations, including the Amorites, who lived in the land. We too will serve the Lord, because he is our God." (Joshua 24:14-18)

Although Joshua and his generation served God, future generations were not so faithful. After the Israelites settled in the Promised

Land, they had a recurring problem with worshipping the idols of the neighboring people, Ba'al and Asherah. It is somewhat puzzling why the Israelites would choose to worship these idols along with God.

The key to understanding this attraction to Ba'al worship is keeping in mind that the Promised Land had an agricultural-based economy. The people depended on adequate rainfall to ensure their survival. Ba'al, who had a female consort named Asherah, was a storm god who brought rain and fertility to the land. The attraction of fertility lured many of the Israelites into Ba'al worship. [4]

Today, in Silicon Valley and nearby areas, the economy is largely based on the development of technology, which has provided many benefits to our society. Most people probably can think of a case or situation in which they have benefited from technology in medicine, business, education or communications. In addition, technology-related companies provide employment for many people.

Although technology has provided many benefits, it can also bring some harm, especially when it takes too much of a dominant place in our society and in people's lives. People can begin to serve technology instead of having it serve them. Technology can become an idol. Here are a few potential hazards of a technology-driven life.

Glued to Mobile Devices

In today's society, many people spend a lot of time on function-rich mobile devices like smart phones. While smart phones provide some benefits, people can become engrossed in their mobile devices in an unhealthy way. Once, I was driving my car on a street that gets a moderate amount of traffic. I approached a crosswalk (with no stop light or stop sign) and saw a man about to cross the street. He was looking at his mobile device and had headphones on. He started to cross the street and all the way across the street, he did not take his eyes off his mobile device. He was totally unaware that

I was there and that I had stopped my car to let him cross the street. Mobile devices can distract people so much that they are not present to their surroundings, other people or God.

Pursuit of Wealth

There is a strong tie between technology and wealth. The high-tech industry draws many people because of the potential for generating wealth. The growth of the high tech industry in the San Francisco Bay Area has made a lot of people rich, but it also has contributed to the high cost of living in the area. Recently, many people have complained about the gentrification of certain neighborhoods in San Francisco, where housing prices have sky-rocketed. A high cost of living hurts the quality of life for people; forcing them to work more, deal with more stress and have less free time. While the high-tech industry provides products to improve the quality of life, it can simultaneously contribute to a decrease in the quality of life in a different way.

High Stress in High-Tech Jobs

Companies in the high-tech industry often try to be on the cutting edge of technology and to create the next hottest product or next popular social media site. Things move at a rapid pace in high-tech, and as a result, jobs are often demanding, fast-paced and stress-producing. High-tech jobs can cause people to feel stressed out and burned out. People may feel that they are giving too much of themselves to their jobs and feel a lack of fulfillment and satisfaction with their careers.

Technology can have a negative impact on people. Therefore, it is important to consider a couple of important questions:

- Is technology serving me or am I serving technology?

- Are technology and the high-tech industry helping me to serve God more effectively or hurting me?

Prayer

> God, I am thankful for the ways that technology has benefited my life. Nevertheless, I do not want to make an idol out of it. I choose to serve God, not technology. Help me not to be blind to the ways that it may be causing damage to my life. Give me the wisdom to use technology in a way that is beneficial to me and your kingdom.

DEVOTION 12
HANDLING REJECTION

If you are waiting to find the right job or the right spouse, one of the most difficult parts of the wait may be handling rejection. When dating, you may think that you finally have found the right person to be your mate, but then that person decides to break up with you. When looking for employment, you may submit many resumes and go through many interviews, but don't receive a job offer. When events like these occur, the pain of rejection often hits people at the core of their beings. The feelings associated with rejection can hurt a person's self-esteem and make it difficult for them to move forward with confidence. Therefore, it is important to learn to deal with rejection in a healthy way.

The first thing to remember is that Jesus knows how it feels to be rejected. Jesus was the perfect Son of God, yet many people rejected him. Jesus experienced the ultimate rejection when the religious leaders arrested him and turned him over to the Roman authorities, who crucified him. Peter, one of Jesus' disciples, referred to Jesus as the living Stone, who is the foundation for our faith:

As you come to him, the living Stone —rejected by humans but chosen by God and precious to him— you also, like living stones, are being built into a spiritual house to be a holy priesthood, offering spiritual sacrifices acceptable to God through Jesus Christ. For in Scripture it says: "See, I lay a stone in Zion, a chosen and precious cornerstone, and the one who trusts in him will never be put to shame." (1 Peter 2:4-6)

Peter wrote to believers who, like Jesus, suffered from rejection by people. He reminded the believers that they are precious to God. Also, Peter encouraged the persecuted believers by telling them that even though they experienced the pain and shame of rejection, God was maturing them into a holy priesthood and ultimately would give them honor, not shame.

Our enemy Satan tries to use rejection to shame us or to lead us into self-condemnation. However, God's Word shows us that rejection is a tool that God uses to mature us and strengthen us. When we experience rejection, we can turn to God without shame and receive his comfort, strength and wisdom. God may show us that one or more of the following statements apply to our situation:

The person or job is not a good fit

God has a plan for each person in his kingdom and each living stone has unique personality traits, talents and callings. Sometimes, a seemingly desirable job or mate may not be a good fit for a person. I have pursued jobs and potential mates that I thought were right for me. In retrospect, I saw that the job or person that I wanted so much actually was not such a good fit for me. Rejection can help you to know yourself better and to know what job or person is a good fit for you.

Humans' rejection is God's protection

Although rejection initially causes pain, God may actually be using the rejection to protect you from much greater pain. Perhaps God is preventing you from getting involved in a marriage or a job which might cause major damage to your spiritual, emotional, physical and/or financial well-being. God has a good plan for your life and sometimes uses rejection to prevent you from going down the wrong path.

God wants to transform a certain part of your character or life

God is building us into a holy priesthood and therefore wants us to grow and mature, so that we can have godly character. Sometimes, God uses the sting of rejection to propel us towards making changes in our lives that will move us towards spiritual maturity. When you experience rejection, it is a good idea to ask God if he wants to work on any particular area of your life.

Rejection can seem like a horrible thing. However, remember that we are precious to God, who uses rejection to grow us into a holy priesthood.

Prayer

God, when I feel rejected, help me to hear your voice and not the condemning and shaming voice of the enemy. Thank you that I am precious to you. I ask that you would give me your wisdom and perspective on my situation. Help me to move forward from the rejection, so that I can grow with other believers into a holy priesthood.

DEVOTION 13
THE MOST DIFFICULT WAIT

Perhaps the most difficult aspect of waiting on God occurs when a person feels that God is absent. Although God promises that he will never leave or forsake his children (Hebrews 13:5), people may experience times when they don't sense the presence of God. Jesus experienced this when he went through a horrible crucifixion and waited to die:

Two rebels were crucified with him, one on his right and one on his left. Those who passed by hurled insults at him, shaking their heads and saying, "You who are going to destroy the temple and build it in three days, save yourself! Come down from the cross, if you are the Son of God!" In the same way the chief priests, the teachers of the law and the elders mocked him. "He saved others," they said, "but he can't save himself! He's the king of Israel! Let him come down now from the cross, and we will believe in him. He trusts in God. Let God rescue him now if he wants him, for he said, 'I am the Son of God.'" In the same way the rebels who were crucified with him also heaped insults on him. From noon until three in the afternoon darkness came over all the land. About three in the afternoon Jesus cried out in a loud voice, "Eli, Eli, lema sabachthani?" (which means "My God, my God, why have you forsaken me?"). (Matthew 27:38-46)

Jesus experienced the most difficult wait. He suffered from not only the physical pain of crucifixion but also the shame from religious leaders and ordinary criminals. The magnitude of the pain and suffering caused Jesus to feel that God had forsaken him.

Why did God allow Jesus to suffer through such an awful death? Jesus could have just been executed quickly without experiencing the terrible anguish of waiting to die on the cross. However, Isaiah 53:10 tells us that "it was the Lord's will to crush him and cause him to suffer." God had a purpose for Jesus' life – to die for the sins of humanity so that people could be restored into a loving relationship with God. Jesus' suffering showed that he carried the burden of all the sins of humanity, and demonstrated his great love for people. If someone goes through tremendous suffering for your benefit, then you know that person really loves you. The terrible anguish that Jesus experienced when he waited to die shows the magnitude of his love for us.

In addition, Jesus was the ultimate example of a person who demonstrated perseverance. The author of the letter to the Hebrews wrote:

> … let us run with perseverance the race marked out for us, fixing our eyes on Jesus, the pioneer and perfecter of faith. For the joy set before him he endured the cross, scorning its shame, and sat down at the right hand of the throne of God. Consider him who endured such opposition from sinners, so that you will not grow weary and lose heart. (Hebrews 12:1b-3)

If you are waiting on God and do not sense his presence, continue to seek him and remember the great example of Jesus, whose difficult wait demonstrated his great love for you.

Prayer

Jesus, thank you that you love me so much that you were willing to go through the most difficult wait on the cross. Thank you that you endured the most terrible physical, emotional and spiritual suffering so that I could be restored into a loving relationship with God.

DEVOTION 14
DEALING WITH COMPETITION

For several years, I worked at PeopleSoft, a software company which faced stiff competition from Oracle, led by the ultra-competitive Larry Ellison. Eventually, PeopleSoft ceased to exist after Oracle executed a hostile takeover. This type of activity is commonplace in the high-tech world, in which companies aggressively pursue success in a fast-moving marketplace.

How should Christians who work in high-tech think about competition and respond to this environment? Is success really about beating the competition? In order to survive, do we need to compete with others? In his letter to the Romans, the apostle Paul provides some good counsel:

> Therefore, I urge you, brothers and sisters, in view of God's mercy, to offer your bodies as a living sacrifice, holy and pleasing to God—this is your true and proper worship. Do not conform to the pattern of this world, but be transformed by the renewing of your mind. Then you will be able to test and approve what God's will is—his good, pleasing and perfect will. (Romans 12:1-2)

Like it or not, competition is a part of the pattern of this world. If we conform to the values of this competitive world, we can easily be drawn away from God and into pride. In his book *Mere Christianity*, C.S. Lewis writes about competitiveness and pride, which he calls the Great Sin:

...Pride is *essentially* competitive ... Pride gets no pleasure out of having something, only out of having more of it than the next man. We say that people are proud of being rich, or clever, or good-looking, but they are not. They are proud of being richer, or cleverer, or better-looking than others. If everyone else became equally rich, or clever, or good-looking, there would be nothing to be proud about. It is the comparison that makes you proud: the pleasure of being above the rest. [5]

A lifestyle driven by pride and competition leads to a lack of peace. If a person always tries to stay ahead of the competition, they can never rest. The person will have problems waiting on God and knowing God's will.

Over the years, playing tennis has helped me to learn about dealing with competition in a godly way. When I play a match, I size up the strengths and weaknesses of my opponents. However, I try to focus the majority of my attention on my actions being holy and pleasing to God. I pray and try to play my best. I try to exhibit good sportsmanship and avoid getting involved in any kind of gamesmanship. Also, I try not to focus on the outcome of the match. I try to stay in the moment and focus on playing one point at a time. When I start thinking too much about the score, it tends to make me tense and I don't play as well.

In his article "Competition: A Word Not Found in the Bible," Os Hillman, president of Marketplace Leaders, provides some helpful guidance:

We are never to view people or organizations as competition. Faith says I do not have to manipulate outcomes. ... we are simply called to obedience and faithfulness. We are to leave outcomes to God. Do those two things and you will always have provision. [6]

God does not call us to take control of our career and financial security by trying to beat the competition. God calls us to surrender control to him, find our worth in him, love others, live a holy and faithful lifestyle, wait on him and trust that he will provide.

Prayer

> God, I choose to pay less attention to people or organizations that I could see as competition. I focus my attention on you and your calling for me to be obedient and faithful. I give up my control and allow you to be in charge of the outcomes.

DEVOTION 15
TRUSTING GOD WHEN PEOPLE DISAPPOINT YOU

Waiting is especially difficult when another person's actions seemingly have put you in an undesirable situation that you wish would end. Perhaps someone on whom you depended has let you down. Maybe someone at your workplace treated you badly or unfairly, and you lost your job or chose to leave an unhealthy employment situation. While you wait for new opportunities, it is easy to feel anger and resentment towards the people who disappointed you.

In the Old Testament, Joseph faced a situation like this when an official in Egypt threw him into prison because of the official's wife, who falsely accused Joseph of trying to sleep with her. Joseph found himself imprisoned due to the actions of an unscrupulous person, and seemingly had no way to get out. However, Joseph did not develop a bad attitude. Instead, he maintained a strong relationship with God, who granted Joseph favor with the prison warden. The warden made him responsible for all the people held in prison, and Joseph served faithfully. One day, Joseph came in contact with another prisoner, Pharaoh's former cupbearer. This man was troubled because he had a dream and could not find anyone to interpret it. God had given Joseph the ability to interpret dreams so he gave the cupbearer an interpretation of the dream and told him:

Within three days Pharaoh will lift up your head and restore you to your position, and you will put Pharaoh's cup in his hand, just as you used to do when you were his cupbearer. But when all goes well with you, remember me and show me kindness; mention me to Pharaoh and get me out of this prison. I was forcibly carried off from the land of the Hebrews, and even here I have done nothing to deserve being put in a dungeon." (Genesis 40:13-15)

Events unfolded just as Joseph had predicted in his interpretation of the dream. The cupbearer left prison and regained his position as Pharaoh's cupbearer. After that happened, Joseph probably waited with hope day by day for his release from prison. Surely, the cupbearer would remember Joseph and his incredible dream interpretation, and talk to Pharaoh. However, the chief cupbearer forgot about Joseph and did not say anything to Pharaoh. Therefore, Joseph had to continue to live in prison and deal with his memories of the two people who disappointed him.

However, that was not the end of the story. Two years later, God intervened in the situation by giving a dream to Pharaoh, who was greatly troubled when he could not find anyone to interpret it. This situation reminded the cupbearer of what happened in the past with Joseph, and he spoke to Pharaoh: "Then the chief cupbearer said to Pharaoh, "Today I am reminded of my shortcomings." (Genesis 41:9). He told Pharaoh about Joseph, and Pharaoh brought Joseph from the prison to interpret his dream. After Joseph correctly interpreted Pharaoh's dream, Joseph's life took a dramatic turn. He went from being a prisoner to serving Pharaoh as his most trusted official.

During your life, you will probably come into contact with some people who have character flaws, and others who have shortcomings. However, while these people may cause you some pain and perhaps put you in an undesirable situation, they do not control your ultimate destiny. It is important to continue to serve God faithfully in whatever situation he places you. God can override human beings' flaws and shortcomings and bring about the plans that he has for your life. God is trustworthy.

Prayer

> God, thank you that you are in control of my destiny. Help me not to dwell on people who have disappointed or hurt me in the past. I choose to forgive them and to serve you faithfully in whatever assignment you give me. I trust that you will bring about the plans that you have for my life.

DEVOTION 16
TAKING A SABBATH: THE WORK CAN WAIT

During the time I studied at seminary in preparation for full-time ministry, I was quite busy. I worked 20 to 30 hours a week – first at a high-tech job, and later as an intern in a church. Also, I had to take more seminary classes than I wanted to because I had a time limit for finishing my degree. These classes required a lot of study time because of the large amount of reading. In one of the courses that focused on the Old Testament, I had an assignment on keeping the Sabbath, which is one of the Ten Commandments:

> Observe the Sabbath day by keeping it holy, as the Lord your God has commanded you. Six days you shall labor and do all your work, but the seventh day is a Sabbath to the Lord your God. On it you shall not do any work, neither you, nor your son or daughter, nor your male or female servant, nor your ox, your donkey or any of your animals, nor any foreigner residing in your towns, so that your male and female servants may rest, as you do. Remember that you were slaves in Egypt and that the Lord your God brought you out of there with a mighty hand and an outstretched arm. Therefore the Lord your God has commanded you to observe the Sabbath day. (Deuteronomy 5:12-15)

When Moses gave the Israelites the Sabbath commandment, he encouraged them to remember that God had delivered them from slavery in Egypt. God designed the Sabbath as a day for us to take a rest from work, so that we can remember what God has done. It is difficult to remember what God has done when we constantly work. It begins to feel that everything depends on our work and that we are in control of our destinies.

After finishing that seminary assignment, I felt convicted that I needed to honor the Sabbath. However, I didn't want to implement this in the manner of the Pharisees, who made up an extensive list of what constituted work and lost the true meaning of the Sabbath. I decided that during a 24-hour period of every week, I would not do any homework or work for my job. During one period of time, I worked at church on Sunday morning and had a seminary class on Monday evening. Therefore, my Sabbath day started on Sunday afternoon and ended on Monday afternoon. With this schedule, I had to plan ahead so that I could finish my homework by Saturday for the Monday evening seminary class. During my Sabbath day, I would not answer work-related emails. I would exercise, go shopping, pray, clean up the house and watch TV. Even though I had a lot of work to do, I found that I could accomplish what I needed to do in six days. In addition, I generally felt rested. After taking a day of rest on a weekly basis, I functioned well. Even after I finished seminary, I continued this habit of taking a Sabbath day.

I learned a simple, but very important lesson while I attended seminary: the work can wait. In the "always connected" high-tech world, people definitely need to understand the importance of a Sabbath day. In the book of Isaiah, God promised a blessing for those who honored the Sabbath:

> "If you keep your feet from breaking the Sabbath and from doing as you please on my holy day, if you call the Sabbath a delight and the Lord's holy day honorable, and if you honor it by not going your own way and not doing as you please or

speaking idle words, then you will find your joy in the Lord, and I will cause you to ride in triumph on the heights of the land and to feast on the inheritance of your father Jacob." The mouth of the Lord has spoken. (Isaiah 58:13-14)

Prayer

> God, I recognize that you command me to honor the Sabbath and to have a weekly day of rest from my normal work routine. I also understand that you instituted the Sabbath for the benefit of your people. I remember how you have acted on my behalf in the past, and I trust that you will continue to provide for me in the future.

DEVOTION 17
AVOIDING IDENTITY THEFT

With the multitude of financial transactions conducted over the Internet, identity theft has become a huge problem in our society. The US Department of Justice reported that in 2012, approximately 16.6 million people or 7% of all US residents 16 years of age and older were victims of identity theft. [7] Therefore, many wise Internet users take measures to protect their identity – installing security software on their computers, using "strong" passwords, and shredding documents that contain personal information. In today's high-tech world, protecting your identity is extremely important.

The high-tech world also poses another kind of threat to your identity—your identity as a child of God. In the book of Romans, the apostle Paul wrote about the great value of a believer's identity:

> For those who are led by the Spirit of God are the children of God. The Spirit you received does not make you slaves, so that you live in fear again; rather, the Spirit you received brought about your adoption to sonship. And by him we cry, "Abba, Father." The Spirit himself testifies with our spirit that we are God's children. Now if we are children, then we are heirs—heirs of God and co-heirs with Christ, if indeed we share in his sufferings in order that we may also share in his glory. (Romans 8:14-17)

Paul points out something amazing – Spirit-led believers are not only children of God, but also co-heirs with Christ who have a glorious inheritance. Believers have a position of security in God's family and don't have to live in fear.

However, the high-tech workplace often puts pressure on people to work many hours and to get things done quickly in order to produce the next, greatest technology. This fast-paced, high-tech lifestyle can slowly eat away at a person's identity. People can begin to live in fear of falling behind and not keeping up with their company's expectation or the competition. People may feel that they always need to prove themselves and are only as good as the work they do. The danger is that their identity comes from their performance, instead of God.

Sarah Young, the author of the well-known devotional book, Jesus Calling, offers these encouraging words:

> Take time to rest by the wayside, for I (Jesus) am not in a hurry. A leisurely pace accomplishes more than hurried striving. When you rush, you forget who you are and Whose you are. Remember that you are royalty in My kingdom [8]

Prayer

> God, in the midst of my busy schedule, I desire to slow down and to root my identity in you. I thank you that through the power of the Holy Spirit, I don't have to live in fear. I can be secure in knowing that I am a child of the awesome God. I thank you that I belong to your family and that I am a co-heir with Christ.

DEVOTION 18

WHERE DOES MY CONFIDENCE AND SELF-ESTEEM COME FROM?

In our competitive world, people find it important to identify and develop their strengths. Each person has strengths from traits that they were born with and from skills and talents developed through practice and work. Often, a person's confidence and self-esteem come in large measure from their strengths.

When waiting on God, these strengths can sometimes seem to be neutralized or devalued. An intelligent, hard working person cannot find a job. A nurturing woman cannot become a parent. During the waiting period, people's strengths may not seem to help or benefit them. Although this experience is painful and difficult, God has a purpose. God often wants to teach people the lesson he taught the apostle Paul.

The apostle Paul had an enviable family background and a great religious education. He had studied under a famous rabbi named Gamaliel and had become a respected religious leader. Then, Paul had an encounter with Jesus, who dramatically changed his life and called him to become a missionary. However, before Paul started his famous missionary journeys, he had a period of waiting which he wrote about in the first chapter of Galatians. During this time, Jesus instructed Paul, who experienced transformation in regards to the source of his confidence and self-esteem. Paul later wrote this:

If someone else thinks they have reasons to put confidence in the flesh, I have more: circumcised on the eighth day, of the people of Israel, of the tribe of Benjamin, a Hebrew of Hebrews; in regard to the law, a Pharisee; as for zeal, persecuting the church; as for righteousness based on the law, faultless.

But whatever were gains to me I now consider loss for the sake of Christ. What is more, I consider everything a loss because of the surpassing worth of knowing Christ Jesus my Lord, for whose sake I have lost all things. I consider them garbage, that I may gain Christ and be found in him, not having a righteousness of my own that comes from the law, but that which is through faith in Christ—the righteousness that comes from God on the basis of faith. (Philippians 3:4-9)

When Paul came to deeply know Jesus Christ and his love, he experienced an inner transformation. He no longer looked to his own strengths and accomplishments to justify himself. His confidence and self-esteem come from knowing and experiencing the love and power of the Lord Jesus Christ. Paul learned to rely on God rather than on his strengths. He gained confidence in the power of God working in and through him.

Paul would later write a powerful prayer for the people in the Ephesian church. If you find yourself waiting on God, this is a good prayer to receive:

I pray that out of his glorious riches he may strengthen you with power through his Spirit in your inner being, so that Christ may dwell in your hearts through faith. And I pray that you, being rooted and established in love, may have power, together with all the Lord's holy people, to grasp how wide and long and high and deep is the love of Christ, and to know this love that surpasses knowledge—that you may be filled to the measure of all the fullness of God.

Now to him who is able to do immeasurably more than all we ask or imagine, according to his power that is at work within us, to him be glory in the church and in Christ Jesus throughout all generations, for ever and ever! Amen. (Ephesians 3:16-21)

During a waiting period, God may uproot the things that you put your confidence in and change the way you look at them. You may come to an understanding that:

- Although you may have worked to develop your strengths, they are gifts from God.
- God did not give you strengths for your personal profit; he gave them to you in order to further his kingdom.
- God's love provides a stronger and more stable foundation for your self-esteem and confidence than your strengths.

Prayer

God, I pray that by the Holy Spirit, you would strengthen me with your power and root me in your deep, deep love. Transform me so that my confidence comes more from your love than from my strengths and abilities. Thank you for the talents and gifts that you have given me. Help me to develop and use them for your kingdom.

DEVOTION 19
THE DANGER OF COMPARISON

Many people enjoy using Facebook to connect and keep up with friends. Active Facebook users post news and pictures about different happenings in their personal lives— their romantic life, career pursuits, vacations, visits to restaurants, and children's accomplishments. In 2014, University of Houston researcher Mai-Ly Steers published an article in the Journal of Social and Clinical Psychology titled, "Seeing Everyone Else's Highlight Reels: How Facebook Usage is Linked to Depressive Symptoms." The results of the study showed that spending a lot of time on Facebook tended to correlate with making comparisons to others and depressed feelings. Steers explained the phenomena:

> ...most of our Facebook friends tend to post about the good things that occur in their lives, while leaving out the bad. If we're comparing ourselves to our friends' "highlight reels," this may lead us to think their lives are better than they actually are and conversely, make us feel worse about our own lives. [9]

A person who feels pressure to live up to high expectations from their family or society may be especially prone to comparing themselves to others. Comparison often leads to envy, which robs people of contentment and peace. The Bible states, "A heart at peace gives life to the body, but envy rots the bones." (Proverbs 14:30)

In a time of waiting, it is especially difficult to avoid comparisons. It may seem that everyone else's life is moving forward except your own. You may be waiting for a spouse and most of your friends have already married. You may be waiting to have a child, and you see pictures of your Facebook friends' children. How can you avoid comparing yourself to others and feeling depressed about your situation? First, it is good to count your blessings by being thankful for the wonderful people and good things that God has put in your life.

Also, it is important to remember that Jesus has a unique plan for your life, just as he did for his disciple, Peter. After Jesus' resurrection, he had a talk with Peter, who had previously denied him three times. Jesus restored Peter, and let him know that he had an important calling – to shepherd God's people. However, Jesus also told Peter that in the future, he would face difficult situations in which he would not be in control. Then, Peter saw John, another one of Jesus' disciples:

When Peter saw him (John), he asked, "Lord, what about him?"

Jesus answered, "If I want him to remain alive until I return, what is that to you? You must follow me." (John 21:21-22)

Jesus said that his plan for John was really none of Peter's business. Instead of comparing himself to John, Peter should focus on following Jesus and what Jesus had for him.

Jesus does not want you to define yourself by how well you stack up against other people. He desires that you simply follow him. God has a unique plan for your life, and your life journey will look different from other people's journeys. Instead of spending a lot of time on Facebook looking at others' highlight reels, it is better to seek God's face and read God's book. This will help you to look forward with joy and hope to what God will do in your life.

Prayer

God, I turn away from comparing myself with other people. Help me to focus my attention on you and what you have for me. Thank you that you have a unique calling and journey for my life.

DEVOTION 20
WAITING FOR THE POWER OF THE HOLY SPIRIT

When I was a pastor in San Francisco, a friend introduced me to Andrew Mutana, a pastor from Kenya. During his childhood years, Andrew had experienced despair and extreme poverty as he grew up without knowing his father. However, he met his Heavenly Father, who dramatically changed his life. He went to college and graduated with a degree in Electrical Engineering. After college he worked as an engineer, but God had a different calling for his life – to be a preacher of the gospel to the nations. Therefore, Andrew quit his job to become a full-time minister. God specifically called Andrew to minister to people in the San Francisco Bay Area, so he began to make regular trips to the area.

As we have become friends over the years, I have observed Andrew ministering on different occasions. I also joined Andrew's ministry team on a mission trip to India. It is apparent that God uses Andrew in a powerful way when he ministers. People experience the power of God and receive salvation, healing and freedom from addictions and past wounds. How does Andrew get the power? I'm convinced that it comes from prayer and fasting. Before Andrew does ministry, he spends time with God and receives the power of the Holy Spirit.

In the book of Acts, Jesus told his disciples to wait and receive the power of the Holy Spirit before they did ministry:

On one occasion, while he (Jesus) was eating with them, he gave them this command: "Do not leave Jerusalem, but wait for the gift my Father promised, which you have heard me speak about. For John baptized with water, but in a few days you will be baptized with the Holy Spirit." " ... you will receive power when the Holy Spirit comes on you; and you will be my witnesses in Jerusalem, and in all Judea and Samaria, and to the ends of the earth." (Acts 1:4-5,8)

After Jesus' disciples received power from the Holy Spirit on the day of Pentecost, they became effective witnesses for Jesus. They successfully brought the good news of Jesus not only to people in familiar areas like Jerusalem and Judea, but also to people of different ethnicities in other parts of the world. This wasn't a result of the abilities of the disciples, who were just ordinary people who worked at ordinary jobs. God empowered the disciples through the filling of the Holy Spirit, and they learned to depend on the power of the Holy Spirit. Later in the Book of Acts, God touched them again with the Holy Spirit: "After they prayed, the place where they were meeting was shaken. And they were all filled with the Holy Spirit and spoke the word of God boldly." (Acts 4:31)

When God calls us to do something, it is important not to take on the task out of our human strength and wisdom. When we wait on God during times of prayer, we can receive the filling and power of the Holy Spirit, which will enable us to accomplish the tasks that God has given us.

Prayer

God, I recognize that you use ordinary people to do your ministry through the power of the Holy Spirit. Before I take on any work that you call me to, I wait for you to fill me with the Holy Spirit. Make me an effective witness for you.

DEVOTION 21
WAITING WITH HOPE

In 2015, *Star Wars* fans eagerly anticipated the release of the new movie, *The Force Awakens*. Director J.J. Abrams, who saw *Star Wars* as an 11-year-old in 1977, wanted to retain some of the wonderful characteristics of the original movie:

> It was a kind of reality that was not normally associated with fantasy or science-fiction stories, a level of filmmaking that was not typically associated with the mainstream genre. And it had incredible heart. There was a sweetness to the story that gave the film this palpable sense of hope. [10]

At the beginning of the original *Star Wars*, Luke Skywalker, played by Mark Hamill, lived on a desert planet, yearning for something more in his life. Similarly, *The Force Awakens* features this storyline at the beginning of the movie:

> ... a young woman name Rey, played by Daisy Ridley, sits disconsolately on a dead-end desert planet in the shade of a wrecked AT-AT (All Terrain Armored Transport), waiting for her life to happen. [11]

At the beginning of these movies, Luke Skywalker and Rey struggle to have hope. During a period of waiting on God, a person can experience similar feelings.

In the Old Testament, the book of Second Chronicles describes the fall of Israel to the Babylonians. Despair hit the Israelites when many were forced from their cherished Promised Land into exile in Babylon. The Prophet Isaiah wrote these words of encouragement:

Why do you complain, Jacob? Why do you say, Israel, "My way is hidden from the Lord; my cause is disregarded by my God"? Do you not know? Have you not heard? The Lord is the everlasting God, the Creator of the ends of the earth. He will not grow tired or weary, and his understanding no one can fathom. He gives strength to the weary and increases the power of the weak. Even youths grow tired and weary, and young men stumble and fall; but those who hope in the Lord will renew their strength. They will soar on wings like eagles; they will run and not grow weary, they will walk and not be faint. (Isaiah 40:27-31)

The Israelites found it difficult to wait in hope when their circumstances looked so terrible. It was easy to fall into despair and negativity because they did not have the resources or ability to change the situation. Isaiah reminded the Israelites about the sovereignty and power of the Lord, in whom they could put their hope as they waited for deliverance from Babylon.

When we face a very discouraging situation, it is helpful to detach our hearts and minds from the difficult circumstances to a certain degree. This does not mean that we deny our sadness and hurt. It is important that we express our pain and sadness to God. We can choose not to place our focus on our circumstances, but instead look to God as our ultimate source of hope. When we open our hearts and minds to the Lord, we are in a good place to receive this wonderful prayer from the apostle Paul:

May the God of hope fill you with all joy and peace as you trust in him, so that you may overflow with hope by the power of the Holy Spirit. (Romans 15:13)

Prayer

Thank you God that you understand my circumstances and the places in me that are sad and hurt. Thank you that I can come to you and express my feelings to you. Help me to focus my attention on you and not on my current circumstances. As I wait, I place my hope and trust in you, believing that "those who hope in the Lord will renew their strength." I rest in your joy and peace.

DEVOTION 22
AN INVITATION TO GROW IN GRACE

Silicon Valley is filled with hard-working, high-achieving people who labor long hours to quickly bring new products to market. High-tech employees often work long hours due to the high demands and the need to communicate with people in different parts of the world. While there is nothing wrong with hard work, this type of high-performance career can have a negative impact on a person's relationship with God when it becomes the center of their focus.

Sometimes, hard-working, high-achieving people struggle with truly understanding and living by God's grace. The Bible tells us that we are saved by grace, not by our works or human effort. Salvation is something that is received, not earned. Once we receive the gift of salvation, we should not strive or revert to works in order to make spiritual progress. Peter encouraged believers to "grow in the grace and knowledge of our Lord and Savior Jesus Christ." (2 Peter 3:18)

A person who grows in grace does not remain idle and become unproductive. Jesus exemplified what living by grace entails:

Jesus gave them this answer: "Very truly I tell you, the Son can do nothing by himself; he can do only what he sees his Father doing, because whatever the Father does the Son also does. For the Father loves the Son and shows him all he does. Yes, and he will show him even greater works than these, so that you will be amazed. (John 5:19-20)

This is an amazing passage! Jesus said that he could not perform any works or deeds out of his own effort. He saw what God the Father was doing, and then joined with the Father in that effort. By joining with God, Jesus was empowered to perform many great deeds and miracles. Jesus lived by grace and produced great works through his relationship with God the Father.

God wants people to learn to live by grace like Jesus did. However, if a person continually works long hours in a high-performance environment, it may be difficult for them to do that. Therefore, sometimes God will bring the person out of such of an environment and into a waiting period. During a period of waiting, a person may feel unproductive and uncertain. However, God often uses such a time to teach the person to grow in grace. God wants the person to learn to wait on him and gain awareness of what He is doing in their life.

Living by grace also involves doing work that comes naturally from a person's God-given talents and gifts. During a waiting period, a person may want to re-examine their natural abilities and gifts. Perhaps the person's prior job has not allowed them to express one of their talents or gifts. God may open a different position that will enable the person and their gifts to flourish.

If you are in a period of waiting, consider that God may be giving you an opportunity to grow in grace. As you learn more and more to live by grace, God can make wonderful things happen in your life.

Prayer

God, teach me and guide me to grow in your grace. I choose not to strive or perform. Help me to see what you are doing so that I can join you in your work. Please put me in a position in which I can gracefully use my God-given gifts for your glory.

DEVOTION 23
OVERCOMING SPIRITUAL AMNESIA

After leaving Egypt, the Israelites waited a long time (40 years) to enter the Promised Land. God had done a great miracle for the Israelites when he parted the Red Sea, allowing them to escape captivity in Egypt. God continued to care for the Israelites as they made their journey to the Promised Land. When they faced a crisis regarding food or water, God provided a supernatural solution to their problem. However, the next time that the Israelites faced a difficult situation, they seemingly would forget what God had done in the past and start to grumble. At one point, the Israelites would turn to an idol, a golden calf, even though God had clearly made himself known to them. The behavior of the Israelites caused their leader, Moses, to become frustrated and angry. What was their problem? I believe that they suffered from spiritual amnesia.

At the end of the Israelites' journey to the Promised Land, God performed another miracle that had similarities to the parting of the Red Sea. When the priests carrying the ark of the covenant stepped into the Jordan River, God stopped the upstream water from flowing, which allowed the entire nation of Israel to cross the river and enter the Promised Land. Then, God gave instructions to the new leader of the Israelites, Joshua, who spoke to some of the Israelites:

So Joshua called together the twelve men he had appointed from the Israelites, one from each tribe, and said to them, "Go over before the ark of the Lord your God into the middle of the Jordan. Each of you is to take up a stone on his shoulder, according to the number of the tribes of the Israelites, to serve as a sign among you. In the future, when your children ask you, 'What do these stones mean?' tell them that the flow of the Jordan was cut off before the ark of the covenant of the Lord. When it crossed the Jordan, the waters of the Jordan were cut off. These stones are to be a memorial to the people of Israel forever." (Joshua 4:4-7)

These memorial stones would help the people of Israel to remember the great act that God had performed.

In the midst of a period of waiting, it is easy to forget what God has done in the past and to fall into spiritual amnesia. Therefore, it is helpful to have items like the memorial stones to give people a reminder of what God has done in the past. Many years ago, I began to keep a scrapbook of significant events in which God did something significant in my life. The scrapbook contains printed materials and pictures of:

- Conferences I attended
- Fellowships and churches I belonged to
- Mission trips I went on
- Houses I owned
- Jobs/Church Positions
- My wedding

Each one of the pages in the scrapbook holds a story of something that God did in my life. When I look at the scrapbook, it reminds me of God's goodness and faithfulness, and strengthens my faith. I remember how God has worked in my life and that God has blessings for me in the future.

If you struggle with spiritual amnesia, it may be helpful for you to have some tangible, physical reminders of what God previously has done in your life. These physical reminders can be as simple as pictures that you display somewhere in your home. These "memorial stones" can help you to remember that God is faithful, and to wait on God.

Prayer

> God, help me not to forget your goodness and faithfulness to me. Show me what tangible reminders that I can use to remind me of what you have done for me in the past.

DEVOTION 24
THE BENEFITS OF DELAYED GRATIFICATION

Delayed gratification occurs when a person decides to abstain from something that will make them feel good immediately in order to receive a better or more enduring benefit later. For example, instead of going to many parties, a student focuses on school work so that eventually the student gets a college degree, a desirable job and a good salary. Psychological studies have shown that a person's ability to delay gratification is linked to academic success, physical health, psychological health and social competence. On the other hand, those who do not practice delayed gratification sometimes fall into a pattern of instant gratification and addiction. In her book *Speed: Facing Our Addiction to Fast and Faster – and Overcoming Our Fear of Slowing Down*, Psychologist Stephanie Brown writes:

> The very essence of addiction to anything – drugs, alcohol, sex, work – is the unwinnable struggle between the desire to keep using or doing something that provides some kind of instant gratification and the reality that there are limits to how long such behavior can go on without severe, even lethal consequences. [12]

Brown also points out that our modern technology, which provides quick access to communication, information, shopping and entertainment, tends to feed the desire for instant gratification: "Technology provides the tools for instant gratification in the same way a hypodermic needle provides an efficient delivery mechanism for heroin." [13]

A person who constantly engages in instant gratification is pleasing what the apostle Paul called the flesh, which also can be understood as the sinful or selfish nature:

Do not be deceived: God cannot be mocked. A man reaps what he sows. Whoever sows to please their flesh, from the flesh will reap destruction; whoever sows to please the Spirit, from the Spirit will reap eternal life. Let us not become weary in doing good, for at the proper time we will reap a harvest if we do not give up. Therefore, as we have opportunity, let us do good to all people, especially to those who belong to the family of believers. (Galatians 6:7-10)

Paul's writing shows his belief in the ultimate form of delayed gratification – followers of Jesus choose not to please their own selfish nature so that they will enjoy the reward of eternal life. For Paul, eternal life did not occur just in heaven, where believers experience a wonderful, loving relationship with God and his family. He believed that Christians get to experience some of the benefits of eternal life here on earth through the presence of the Holy Spirit. Therefore, Paul encouraged people to live by the Spirit (Galatians 5:16). Instead of seeking instant gratification in things of this earth, it is better to embrace the presence and guidance of the Holy Spirit, which provides love, peace, comfort and power. The Holy Spirit guides people into a fruitful life, which includes acts of service to help and bless others.

Also, Paul understood that believers often would not see instant results from their good deeds. Therefore, he encouraged the Galatians not to get tired of sowing seeds of goodness, so that they would reap a harvest in the future. This harvest included people who would come to know Jesus Christ and the love of God.

People who struggle with instant gratification and addiction usually end up damaging their relationships with others. If technology provides a person with the tools to engage in instant gratification, it is important for them to consider how to use technology wisely. It may be helpful to sometimes turn off all mobile devices and spend time praying and waiting for the guidance of the Holy Spirit. God desires that people pursue a Spirit-led life and be free from the need for instant gratification. In this God-given freedom, people can sow seeds to bless others and experience the benefits of eternal life.

Prayer

> God, free me from the need for instant gratification and pleasing my "flesh." Give me the strength to turn away from any addictive behaviors. Guide me through the Holy Spirit to use technology wisely and to please you, so that many others can come to know Jesus and experience eternal life.

DEVOTION 25
WAITING FOR GOD IN WORSHIP

Currently, one of my favorite worship songs is *Waiting Here For You,* written by Chris Tomlin, Jesse Reeves and Martin Smith, and sung by worship leader Christy Nockels. This song has similarities to Psalm 33, a hymn that starts with these words of exhortation for the congregation and the musicians (verses 1-3):

Sing joyfully to the Lord, you righteous;
  it is fitting for the upright to praise him.
Praise the Lord with the harp;
  make music to him on the ten-stringed lyre.
Sing to him a new song;
  play skillfully, and shout for joy.

The middle section of the psalm includes these words, which point to the God's power and plans (verses 6-11):

By the word of the Lord the heavens were made,
  their starry host by the breath of his mouth.
He gathers the waters of the sea into jars;
  he puts the deep into storehouses.
Let all the earth fear the Lord;
  let all the people of the world revere him.
For he spoke, and it came to be;
  he commanded, and it stood firm.
The Lord foils the plans of the nations;
  he thwarts the purposes of the peoples.
But the plans of the Lord stand firm forever,

the purposes of his heart through all generations.

The hymn ends with these words of response from the congregation (verses 20-22):

> We wait in hope for the Lord;
>> he is our help and our shield.
> In him our hearts rejoice,
>> for we trust in his holy name.
> May your unfailing love be with us, Lord,
>> even as we put our hope in you.

This psalm shows a progression during a time of worshiping God. At the beginning, God's people are encouraged to enter into the worship experience and to engage with God through musical expression. The musicians are encouraged to play their instruments and the congregation is instructed to sing to God. This helps the congregation to begin to focus its attention on God and to draw near to God. Often, in our busy world, many things grab our attention and clutter our minds. When we worship God, we turn our hearts and minds to God.

As the worship continues, the congregation worships God for who He is – the Lord of all creation and the ruler of the earth. The congregation focuses on God's power and sovereign plans. As we go about our daily lives, we can easily lose sight of this. We need a reminder of God's rightful place in our lives. Worship helps to bring our lives into a proper perspective as we have a sense of awe and wonder about God.

Unlike the beginning, the later part of the worship is not so expressive. The congregation takes a posture of waiting expectantly for God. The song *Waiting Here for You* contains these lyrics: "We come with expectation, waiting here for you." [14] As we wait, we can experience the presence of God, which comforts us and helps us to trust God. Sometimes, we may hear a word of encouragement or guidance from God.

I have found it very helpful to have personal times of worship. I play guitar, praise God and wait for God to speak to me. During these times, I experience God's presence and hear his words of guidance for different situations in my life. When we worship God, corporately or privately, it is good to spend some time waiting expectantly for God.

Prayer

God, my desire is that my worship is pleasing to you and not just a routine. I want to worship with a sense of awe and expectancy. I turn my attention away from all the things that clutter my mind and wait for you. Thank you for your wonderful presence.

DEVOTION 26
THE IMPORTANCE OF BEING PRESENT

After I delivered a sermon in which I spoke about technology, a person from the congregation came to talk to me about something she had experienced. She was taking BART (rapid transit) to San Francisco and had to make a transfer. As she waited for a train, she was surprised by the silence at the station. It was so quiet that she could hear a car door being closed in the parking lot. There were groups of people who knew each other, but they were not having conversations. Instead of having social interaction, they were engaged in social media or other things that their smartphones offer—the Internet, video games or a text message exchange. After this experience, she realized how much of a hold that technology has on people.

Technology can help people connect with each other. It's great that I can use Skype on my iPhone to talk to my wife Jill while she is overseas. However, in many cases, technology absorbs people so much that they don't focus on relating with the people around them. When this happens, people miss out on something very important. In his book, *Christian Coaching*, Gary Collins writes about a young man who needs more social interaction:

> Kevin is one of my neighbors, a young man who works in a computer software company where his superior knowledge and technical skills have brought affirmation from his employer and respect from his coworkers. In spite of his capabilities, Kevin's career seems to be stalled. The problem has nothing to do with his work. According to his supervisor,

Kevin has missed promotions because he lacks the ability to relate comfortably to people. [15]

Kevin, like many people in Silicon Valley, is not lacking in technological competence. However, he needs to improve on what Gary Collins refers to in his book as social intelligence. A person with high social intelligence knows the importance of being present to other people. To be fully present to people, we cannot be like the people at the BART station. We need to intentionally turn off or silence our technological devices and focus our attention on people. Here are some of the characteristics of a person who is present for other people:

- Is not distracted and focuses their full attention on the other person.
- Listens well to what the other person is saying.
- Asks good questions to show an interest in the other person.
- Is able to carry a spontaneous conversation.
- Empathizes and shows concern.
- Is sensitive to and is in tune with the other person's emotions.
- Develops a connection with the other person.

I believe that being present is an important part of loving people. In his letter to the Roman church, the apostle Paul wrote:

Love must be sincere. Hate what is evil; cling to what is good. Be devoted to one another in love. Honor one another above yourselves. Never be lacking in zeal, but keep your spiritual fervor, serving the Lord. Be joyful in hope, patient in affliction, faithful in prayer. Share with the Lord's people who are in need. Practice hospitality. Bless those who persecute you; bless and do not curse. Rejoice with those who rejoice; mourn with those who mourn. Live in harmony with one another. Do not be proud, but be willing to associate with people of low position. Do not be conceited. (Romans 12:9-16)

When we are present for other people, we are truly able to "rejoice with those who rejoice; mourn with those who mourn." We can be "in tune" with other people and what they are experiencing in their lives. If you are waiting to move forward in getting a promotion, finding a marriage partner or ministering to people, it is a good idea to use your mobile device less and learn to be present to people more.

Prayer

God, I desire to be present to you and to the people around me. Give me the wisdom to know when to turn off or put away my mobile device. Grow me in my ability to connect with and be present to other people.

DEVOTION 27
BE CAREFUL WITH OPEN DOORS

During a time of waiting, a person sometimes hears these words of encouragement – "God will open a door for you." The apostle Paul wrote about the concept of an open door in a letter to the church at Corinth:

> After I go through Macedonia, I will come to you—for I will be going through Macedonia. Perhaps I will stay with you for a while, or even spend the winter, so that you can help me on my journey, wherever I go. For I do not want to see you now and make only a passing visit; I hope to spend some time with you, if the Lord permits. But I will stay on at Ephesus until Pentecost, because a great door for effective work has opened to me, and there are many who oppose me. (1 Corinthians 16:5-9)

In this case, Paul decided to delay his visit to Corinth and take the open door in Ephesus, despite the presence of opposition. In other situations during his ministry, Paul had faced opposition and decided to move on, believing that the door to ministry had closed. How did Paul know that God had opened a door for him in this particular case? We cannot be sure how he knew this. However, it seems likely that Paul used good wisdom and discernment.

Sometimes, an apparent open door is not from God. By going through the door, a person can take the wrong path and later experience problems and pain. When waiting on God, it is very important to have good wisdom and discernment. Wisdom is especially important when making long term commitments in relationships, business, ministry and real estate. Charles Stanley writes about the importance of discernment for singles who want to get married:

> Certainly, many of the Christian singles I've known over the years would acknowledge that, in theory, no person can meet all their needs. They would agree that only God can satisfy their deepest longings. But how they act is a different manner. And when they meet another person who is willing to tie the knot, I've sadly seen many of them rush into the union without much discernment. They don't consult the Father, ensuring that this is the person He has in mind for them. Their prayers are based on keeping their boyfriend or girlfriend happy, rather than seeking God's will. Ultimately, however, they want just one thing – and that's to ease their loneliness. Now what they're really longing for is true intimacy – genuine oneness of heart and spirit that the Father intended for the marriage relationship. But because they are tired of waiting, they settle for sex and a false sense of security. And what they reap are problems and devastating heartbreak. [16]

In life, we all make mistakes, but not all mistakes are equal. Some mistakes cause major pain and may not be reversible. Therefore, it is important to develop good wisdom and discernment in order to avoid making major and catastrophic mistakes. The author of Proverbs wrote about the importance of wisdom:

For the Lord gives wisdom;
   from his mouth come knowledge and understanding.
He holds success in store for the upright,
   he is a shield to those whose walk is blameless,

for he guards the course of the just
    and protects the way of his faithful ones.
Then you will understand what is right and just
    and fair—every good path.
For wisdom will enter your heart,
    and knowledge will be pleasant to your soul.
Discretion will protect you,
    and understanding will guard you. (Proverbs 2:6-11)

Here are some guidelines for discerning if an open door is from God:

Take time to pray and discern.

Sometimes, a person's emotions may lead them to make a quick decision about an apparent open door. It is important to take time to read applicable passages from the Bible, pray and discern God's will in the matter. A good question to ask yourself is "Did I hear God say to go through this open door?"

Seek godly counsel from a pastor, spiritual leader, mentor or coach.

It is important to tell your whole story to a spiritual leader and to give careful consideration to the counsel from the leader. The spiritual leader may be able to give you a different perspective that will help to bring greater clarity to your situation.

Do some further investigation.

If you don't have clear direction from God, it likely is a good idea to delay the decision and do some further investigation. During this time, you wait on God to show you more. The investigation could involve bringing other people into the decision making process. If the decision involves a job, the discernment process could involve another meeting with the employer.

During the discernment process, God may close the door or show you that it is not really an open door. On the other hand, God may show you that it is his open door for you. By consulting God and using good discernment, you will feel more confident in moving forward.

Prayer

> God, when I have a possible open door, help me not to be guided too much by my emotions. I choose to wait on you, seek your wisdom and discernment, and carefully consider the counsel of the spiritual leaders in my life.

DEVOTION 28
TIMES OF WAITING ARE OFTEN TIMES OF TRAINING

Companies in a variety of industries have their Information Technology (IT) departments implement new computer systems to make their businesses run more efficiently and effectively. When I worked in high-tech, some of my work involved implementing new computer systems or developing training materials for new systems. One of the keys to successful implementations is training employees on the new system. People tend to be comfortable with the familiar, old system, and sometimes are reluctant to move to something new. Therefore, companies need to invest in training for their employees. This involves taking people away from their day-to-day work and spending time and money to train them on the new system. Although one can view training as not being productive work, it is essential to the long-term success of the implementation.

Training is also important when God has a new assignment for our lives. There are times when God has something new and exciting for us. It could be a new job, a new ministry, a promotion, or a new relationship – to be a spouse or a parent. Although we often want the new assignment immediately, it can be beneficial to wait and allow God to have some time to train, develop and mature us. This was certainly true in the lives of two kings of Israel: Saul and David.

The Bible does not paint a kind picture of Saul and his reign as the king. At certain points in his life, Saul did not follow God and took ungodly actions. After looking at the Bible narrative about Saul's installation and early days as the king, I have some compassion for him because he did not receive the proper training to be a leader. Saul was unprepared to be the king when the people of Israel demanded that the nation be led by a king so that Israel could be like all other nations. The former leader of Israel, Samuel, anointed Saul with oil and later, the Spirit of God came upon Saul. Immediately, Saul began his reign as the king and the Spirit of God impacted him positively as he showed courage in a conflict with the Ammonites (1 Samuel 11). However, shortly after that, Saul faltered when he faced a potential conflict with the Philistines (1 Samuel 13). At this time, his troops became afraid and began to scatter. Instead of going to God for direction, Saul took matters into his own hands and made a burnt offering to God, something that only priests were allowed to do. When Samuel arrived, he told Saul that he had "acted foolishly." During his reign as the king, Saul continued to make errors and not follow the Lord's direction. Although Saul had received the Spirit of God, he lacked the proper training and spiritual formation to develop into a godly king.

On the other hand, David had time with God for training and preparation for his role as king. When Samuel anointed David as the future king, he was a young man (probably a teenager) who looked after his father's sheep. At this point in time, David received the anointing and power of the Holy Spirit, but he did not become the king for many years. During this period of waiting, God trained David, who continued to work part-time as a shepherd. Although shepherding work was not glamourous, it provided essential training that David would need later. When David faced a conflict with Goliath, a Philistine, he drew upon his experiences with God during his shepherding work:

David said to Saul, "Let no one lose heart on account of this Philistine; your servant will go and fight him."

Saul replied, "You are not able to go out against this Philistine and fight him; you are only a young man, and he has been a warrior from his youth."

But David said to Saul, "Your servant has been keeping his father's sheep. When a lion or a bear came and carried off a sheep from the flock, I went after it, struck it and rescued the sheep from its mouth. When it turned on me, I seized it by its hair, struck it and killed it. Your servant has killed both the lion and the bear; this uncircumcised Philistine will be like one of them, because he has defied the armies of the living God. The Lord who rescued me from the paw of the lion and the paw of the bear will rescue me from the hand of this Philistine."

Saul said to David, "Go, and the Lord be with you." (1 Samuel 17:32-37)

David gained experience with the power of God during his shepherding days. David killed two ferocious animals, apparently with his bare hands! These experiences gave him confidence and boldness in the power of God when he faced the intimidating Goliath, whom he defeated. The period of waiting for David was not wasted time. Times of waiting are often times of training.

Prayer

God, as I wait for the new assignment that you have for me, I choose to make good use of the time. Help me to learn the lessons that you want to teach me. Thank you that you are preparing me for what is next in my life.

DEVOTION 29
THE CAREER CAN WAIT

In September 2014, Patrick Tang, a director at a well-established high-tech company, decided to go to the Philippines to visit the child that he and his wife had sponsored for ten years through Compassion International. He journeyed to the village in the Iloilo province and found that the villagers lived in simple bamboo shacks with tin roofs. Less than a year before Patrick visited, Typhoon Yolanda had hit the Philippines and destroyed a couple of the houses in the village. After Patrick spent a half of a rainy day with his sponsored child, he left to go back to his hotel. At this time, God put a deep impression on his heart: "You are going back to the comfort of your hotel. They are walking back through the muddy village. What are you going to do about it?"

Patrick felt that God wanted him to help the village build some typhoon-resistant housing. However, he didn't know where to start because he had no background in civil engineering. Despite Patrick's doubts, he began to do some investigation and God put some people in his path that would help the project move forward. While at an airport on a business trip to China, he met an American who had gone to the Philippines to repair church buildings. This man provided Patrick with useful information and encouragement. Then, Patrick took another trip to the village to find out if a building project was feasible. He spent time getting to know the villagers and sharing the vision that God gave him. At a village elder meeting, the matriarch of the village granted some land for building a typhoon-resistant community hall. Bolstered by the support of the village, Patrick returned to the United States and considered his next steps. He felt a strong calling from God that he needed to do this project even though he had an important job in Silicon Valley.

Patrick's situation was similar to the circumstances that Nehemiah faced when he served the king of Persia. Nehemiah found out from his brother about the distress of the Jewish people in Jerusalem, which no longer had a functioning wall to protect it. During a time of prayer and fasting, Nehemiah felt called to take action to fix the broken-down wall. He then prayed about approaching the king about his idea:

"Lord, let your ear be attentive to the prayer of this your servant and to the prayer of your servants who delight in revering your name. Give your servant success today by granting him favor in the presence of this man."

I was cupbearer to the king.

In the month of Nisan in the twentieth year of King Artaxerxes, when wine was brought for him, I took the wine and gave it to the king. I had not been sad in his presence before, so the king asked me, "Why does your face look so sad when you are not ill? This can be nothing but sadness of heart."

I was very much afraid, but I said to the king, "May the king live forever! Why should my face not look sad when the city where my ancestors are buried lies in ruins, and its gates have been destroyed by fire?"

The king said to me, "What is it you want?"

> Then I prayed to the God of heaven, and I answered the king,
> "If it pleases the king and if your servant has found favor in his
> sight, let him send me to the city in Judah where my ances-
> tors are buried so that I can rebuild it." (Nehemiah 1:11-2:5)

The king not only granted Nehemiah permission to rebuild the wall, but also provided timber for the project.

Just as Nehemiah had to push through his fear and approach the king, Patrick decided to talk to his manager and ask for a sabbatical. Patrick had determined that he didn't want to make career success into an idol. Therefore, he decided that whether or not his manager gave permission, he was going to pursue the project in the Philippines. If his manager did not grant him permission, he would give up his job. He trusted that God would later lead him to a job that would provide for the needs of his wife and two children.

After Patrick talked to his manager, the company decided to grant him permission to take a sabbatical for the project in the Philippines. God had clearly made a way for Patrick to go forward with the work in the Philippines, which he named Project Mustard Seed (https://growingmustardseeds.wordpress.com). Patrick hired a local architect, and the building of the typhoon-resistant community hall started in July, 2015. Since then, the vision of Project Mustard Seed has expanded to include:

- Providing college scholarships.

- Helping new businesses get started.

- Partnering with local churches to disciple people.

Not only did Patrick keep his job at his company after he returned from the Philippines but he also received a promotion!

If God calls you to do something that seems too difficult and requires you to give up the security of your job or career, pray and ask God to increase and strengthen your faith. God can provide and do much more than what we think is possible.

Prayer

> God, I choose not to make an idol out of my career. I desire to use some of the resources and time that you have given me to help and bless other people. Open the door for me to minister to people and further your kingdom.

DEVOTION 30

WAITING FOR A HOUSE: A BLESSING IN DISGUISE

In Jesus' well-known Sermon on the Mount, he exhorted the audience to prioritize God's kingdom and their relationship with God above the consideration of their own needs. Jesus reminded them that they have a good Father who provides for their needs:

> "And why do you worry about clothes? See how the flowers of the field grow. They do not labor or spin. Yet I tell you that not even Solomon in all his splendor was dressed like one of these. If that is how God clothes the grass of the field, which is here today and tomorrow is thrown into the fire, will he not much more clothe you—you of little faith? So do not worry, saying, 'What shall we eat?' or 'What shall we drink?' or 'What shall we wear?' For the pagans run after all these things, and your heavenly Father knows that you need them. But seek first his kingdom and his righteousness, and all these things will be given to you as well." (Matthew 6:28-33)

Although Jesus only spoke specifically about food and clothing, I have come to understand that this scripture has a broader scope. If we apply this scripture to our current American society and in particular the San Francisco Bay Area, then real estate enters the discussion. Due to the high price of real estate and a tight supply of house in the Bay Area, many people put tremendous effort into acquiring a home. Jesus' words remind us to focus our attention on God's kingdom and to trust that God will provide.

I sold my house in Fremont in 2004 when I moved to another area to work as an intern in a church. During the ensuing years, the housing market became extremely hot and prices skyrocketed. In 2006, I began to serve as an associate pastor in San Francisco and rented a small one-bedroom apartment. I hoped that someday I could purchase another home because when I owned a home, I found that productive ministry occurred when I invited people to my house. However, with my salary, it didn't look like I could afford to purchase another house in the inflated real estate market. So I waited.

Then, in 2008, the financial crisis occurred, and real estate prices dropped significantly. I decided to look for a house in San Bruno, a city ten miles south of San Francisco where the housing prices were somewhat lower. I hoped to find a basic three-bedroom house with a large enough living room to host people from my church. Even though prices had dropped, I had difficulty finding a suitable house that I could afford. I felt that the houses that I could afford were not worth the price.

While searching the Internet, I found a house that was a short sale. Although the house had been on the market for about nine months and the sellers had reduced the listing price by over 15%, the price still exceeded my budget. However, I decided to contact my real estate agent and we went to look at the house. In addition to featuring three bedrooms and an office, the house had a fairly large living room. When we went into the kitchen, we noticed that the previous owner had put in new appliances. However, the kitchen had somewhat of a bad smell. When I opened the door of the refrigerator, I found out what caused this smell. There was something growing on the walls of the refrigerator, which produced an incredibly nasty, horrible smell. I quickly shut the refrigerator door, but the smell disturbed my real estate agent so much that she could not stay in the kitchen.

I had a discussion with my real estate agent about why the house had been on the market for nine months, and no one had purchased it at the reduced price. She didn't see any major problems with the house. Therefore, despite the smelly refrigerator, I proceeded to put in a low offer that was below the asking price. The bank accepted the offer, and the inspection reports didn't reveal any major red flags with the house. I moved forward with the purchase and felt fortunate to get a better house than I thought that I could afford. After I took ownership of the house, I purchased a new refrigerator from Lowe's. A delivery man came with my new refrigerator and hauled away the smelly one. Soon after that, I purchased a new stove because I found that the one in the kitchen did not work. The same Lowe's delivery man delivered the new stove and told me that when he hauled away my refrigerator, it stunk up his truck! Later, I met my next door neighbor, who told me that one of her friends had considered purchasing the house I bought. However, her friend decided not to buy the house because of the bad smell in the kitchen. The smelly refrigerator allowed me to purchase a house that I could not have afforded. I'll always believe that the smelly refrigerator was a blessing in disguise from God.

Prayer

God, thank you that you are a heavenly Father who takes care of my needs for clothing, food and housing. I understand that you don't want me to worry, but instead to put my trust in you. I make your kingdom a priority, believing that you will take care of me.

DEVOTION 31
THE IMPORTANCE OF REAL, NON-VIRTUAL RELATIONSHIPS

In her book *Speed: Facing Our Addiction to Fast and Faster—And Overcoming Our Fear of Slowing Down*, Stephanie Brown expresses concern about how people form relationships in the Silicon Valley high-tech culture. Instead of having relationships based on face-to-face meetings that involve emotional engagement, the culture has moved towards relationships based on interactions via social media. Brown defines these as virtual relationships, in which communication occurs solely through the internet or mobile devices (e-mail, texting and social media). Brown points out the down side:

When you evaluate your worth by your number of social media friends and shift the method of building friendships to quick, short hits on the "Accept" or "Like" buttons, you change the nature of friendship. Without emotional engagement, you are left with a virtual list of contacts, not friends. Instead of a few long-term close friends and even your most intimate partner, you gather superficial, short encounters.

No wonder so many people feel lonely and deeply unfulfilled in their relationships. Many say they don't know how to establish an intimate bond or they don't have time anymore. Young people often have no idea of what an intimate, open, vulnerable, and trusting relationship is. They think human relationship is a commodity. You shop for friends and you market yourself. We have radically shifted our deepest understanding of what constitutes closeness, commitment, and connection. We are paying a huge price already and it will get worse. We are eliminating our value of being real in the drive for image enhancement in the pursuit of success. [17]

Social media and online communication have provided some real benefits to human relationships. Facebook allows you to keep up with a wider circle of friends and let others know what you are doing. Also, online dating has provided a vehicle through which many couples have met. Prior to meeting my wife Jill, I tried online dating through an introduction from a friend. Although online dating helped me to connect with some women who had similar values and interests, I found that until I actually had a face-to-face interaction with a woman, I didn't know if we had good chemistry or might be a good fit for each other.

There is no substitute for real, non-virtual relationships. God made us to be in relationship with not only him, but also with family and friends. These words from the book of Ecclesiastes in the Old Testament are very applicable to our culture today:

Again I saw something meaningless under the sun:
There was a man all alone;
   he had neither son nor brother.
There was no end to his toil,
   yet his eyes were not content with his wealth.
"For whom am I toiling," he asked,
   "and why am I depriving myself of enjoyment?"
This too is meaningless—
   a miserable business!

Two are better than one,
   because they have a good return for their labor:

If either of them falls down,
> one can help the other up.
But pity anyone who falls
> and has no one to help them up.
Also, if two lie down together, they will keep warm.
> But how can one keep warm alone?
Though one may be overpowered,
> two can defend themselves.
A cord of three strands is not quickly broken. (Ecclesiastes 4:7-12)

We need more than virtual connections in order to be relationally healthy. We need people to walk with us as we go through life, in which we often face difficulties, disappointments and changes. In our fast-paced, success-oriented culture filled with mobile devices, it is important to take the time and effort to develop real relationships.

Prayer

> Father, I desire to have real, non-virtual relationships. I want my social media activity to augment my relational life but not be my main way of relating to others. I choose to make time to have real connection with other people. Teach me how to build healthy, supportive relationships with others.

DEVOTION 32
FINDING CONTENTMENT DURING A WAITING PERIOD

In the Roman Empire, slaves played an important role in the economy. Through military conquests, the Romans captured many foreigners and turned them into slaves. Although many slaves were unskilled, others had received education and worked at skilled jobs as teachers, accountants and physicians. Some slaves could earn wages or an allowance, and in a small number of cases, might save enough money to purchase their freedom from their masters. Freed slaves who had belonged to a Roman citizen could even become citizens themselves and gain the right to vote.

As Christianity spread in the Roman Empire, a number of slaves became followers of Jesus. Slaves found the Christian church attractive because it offered them equal status with free people. In his first letter to the church in Corinth, the apostle Paul gave some counsel to slaves:

> Nevertheless, each person should live as a believer in whatever situation the Lord has assigned to them, just as God has called them. This is the rule I lay down in all the churches.

> Were you a slave when you were called? Don't let it trouble you—although if you can gain your freedom, do so. For the one who was a slave when called to faith in the Lord is the Lord's freed person; similarly, the one who was free when called is Christ's slave. (1 Corinthians 7:17, 21-22)

Certainly, most slaves wanted to change their social and economic standing by gaining their freedom. Paul validated their desire for freedom by telling them that they should gain their freedom if it was possible. However, he told the slaves not to become troubled if they could not change their social status. In other words, the slaves should accept their position and be content in their situation. They should not expend too much energy trying to become free. Instead, slaves should rejoice in their freedom in Christ. Although they did not have freedom in their society, they possessed a different kind of freedom – an internal freedom from the bondage of sin.

This passage contains some helpful wisdom for those who struggle with contentment during a waiting period. Although a person in a waiting period feels some discontentment with their present circumstances, they will find it beneficial to accept their current situation and find joy in their relationship with God. Not accepting the current circumstances takes away a person's peace and happiness. At the same time, it is not healthy to become resigned to the circumstances and not take any action to move forward. As Paul wrote to the slaves, if you can change your circumstances, go ahead and do so.

Also, it is important to remember that although the grass may look greener on the other side, there are also challenges on the other side. Paul pointed out to slaves that people who have freedom in the society are actually Christ's slaves. "Free" believers cannot do whatever they want. They come under the lordship of Jesus and follow him wherever He leads them in this world.

Immediately after Paul addressed slaves in 1 Corinthians, he wrote to unmarried people. Single people sometimes feel that their problems and struggles would be solved if they only would have a marriage partner. Paul affirmed single people's desire to marry but pointed out that "those who marry will face many troubles in this life..." (1 Corinthians 7:28). There are challenges and problems in life regardless of our particular circumstances. Therefore, it is best to find contentment in whatever situation the Lord has assigned to us.

Prayer

God, although the grass may look greener on the other side, I recognize that there will be challenges and difficulties in all situations in life. Although I struggle with my current circumstances, I accept them because you have assigned them to me for this season of my life. Help me to find a healthy sense of contentment and to walk faithfully with you.

DEVOTION 33
EDUCATION: A GOOD THING THAT CAN BECOME AN IDOL

My wife Jill and I like to go on walks in our neighborhood in the Irvington district of Fremont. One day, we noticed a house that had streamers with Chinese characters on the right and left sides of the front door. As we walked closer to the house, I asked Jill what the characters on the streamers meant. She told me that it basically said, "We have come a long way from China so that our children can get a good education and succeed." The content of the streamers did not shock me. In the Irvington District, this emphasis on good education and success is quite common. Irvington High School is ranked in the top 5% of all high schools in California. [18]

However, I was a little surprised that the homeowner would display such a public and visible statement about their goals on their house. What came to my mind was a passage from the Old Testament in which Moses encouraged the Israelites to write something very important on their doorframes:

> Hear, O Israel: The Lord our God, the Lord is one. Love the Lord your God with all your heart and with all your soul and with all your strength. These commandments that I give you today are to be on your hearts. Impress them on your children. Talk about them when you sit at home and when you walk along the road, when you lie down and when you get up. Tie them as symbols on your hands and bind them on your

foreheads. **Write them on the doorframes of your houses** and
on your gates. (Deuteronomy 6:4-9)

In the previous chapter, Moses had spoken to the Israelites about the
Ten Commandments, which would form the basis for the new nation
of Israel. Moses believed that these commandments were so important
that he wanted the Israelites to have a highly visible reminder of them
every time they went in and out of their houses.

There is no doubt that getting a good education is a good thing.
However, when a good thing becomes the center of attention at the
expense of God, then the good thing becomes an idol. Dr. Tim Keller,
pastor of Redeemer Presbyterian Church in Manhattan, states:

> We think that idols are bad things, but that is almost never the
> case. The greater the good, the more likely we are to expect that
> it can satisfy our deepest needs and hopes. Anything can serve
> as a counterfeit god, especially the very best things in life. [19]

When educational success becomes the ultimate goal rather than
preparation for God's plan for a person's life, then problems begin to
occur. For example, pursuing success in the American educational
system may be dangerous to the development of good character in students. Research has showed that cheating in schools has risen greatly
over the past 50 years. An Educational Testing Service/Ad Council
fact sheet reports that between 75% and 98% of college students admit
that they cheated while in high school. This fact sheet points out that
"Less social disapproval coupled with increased competition for admis-
sion into universities and graduate schools has made students more
willing to do whatever it takes to get the A." [20] When a degree from a
top university becomes the highest priority and God's value system is
ignored, then there is a huge cost – a decline of good character in our
students and our society. I believe that education needs to be put in its

proper place – as a good thing that helps people to fulfill God's plan for their lives.

Getting a degree from an excellent university does not necessarily help a person to know their purpose in life. At a conference, I met a young adult who had worked hard, performed well in school, and landed a good job with a start-up company. However, this young adult felt pressure to work a lot of hours at an unsatisfying job. Education had helped the young adult to get a good job, but it did not bring fulfillment.

The apostle Paul wrote, "For we are God's handiwork, created in Christ Jesus to do good works, which God prepared in advance for us to do." (Ephesians 2:10). When we are in relationship with Christ Jesus, we can better understand how God made us and move towards the purpose that God has planned for us. This process of knowing your God-given purpose is very different from getting an educational degree. When you are working towards a degree, you know what you need to do to get good grades and the degree. You are largely in control of moving towards your goal. Finding your God-given purpose is quite different. It involves a journey with God in which you allow God to lead you and shape you. Sometimes you have to wait on God. Along the way, you come to know God and yourself better, and understand how God can use your life experiences, education, gifts and talents to fulfill his purpose for your life. This is something worth waiting for.

Prayer

> God, I recognize that an education degree from a highly-ranked college is a good thing, but it does not guarantee success or satisfaction in life. I declare that educational success will not be an idol in my household. Help me to use my education to fulfill your purpose for my life.

DEVOTION 34
THE VIRTUE OF PATIENCE

In his freshman year, Stanford running back Christian McCaffrey had some success on the football field by utilizing his great speed to run away from opponents. In McCaffrey's sophomore year, he had a breakout season and became a contender for the prestigious Heisman Trophy award. One sportswriter took notice of improvements that he had made:

> The 6-foot, 201-pound sophomore is more self-assured and stronger, sure. He also is more patient. Instead of trying to force plays, McCaffrey has perfected how to wait between his tackles until the precise moment when a hole appears. [21]

McCaffrey's assets include a combination of speed and patience that has helped him to excel in different circumstances on the football field. It is interesting to watch someone who has developed both speed and patience because typically, those two things don't go together.

Our modern, high-tech society greatly values speed but tends not to place importance on patience. People want quick access to the Internet and fast download speeds. E-mail is not fast enough, so some people avoid it and instead use texting. Some people try to find relationships through speed dating. High-tech companies want to get new products to market rapidly. With this emphasis on speed, people tend to want responses and results right away. Technology has made great contributions to our society, but also influences people to disregard the virtue of patience. People without patience sometimes rush into making poor choices and decisions, give up too quickly, or treat people poorly.

Patience is a virtuous trait that God exhibits to people. The apostle Paul greatly appreciated Jesus' patience:

> Here is a trustworthy saying that deserves full acceptance: Christ Jesus came into the world to save sinners—of whom I am the worst. But for that very reason I was shown mercy so that in me, the worst of sinners, Christ Jesus might display his immense patience as an example for those who would believe in him and receive eternal life. (1 Timothy 1:15-16)

Paul also encouraged believers to develop the virtue of patience:

> Therefore, as God's chosen people, holy and dearly loved, clothe yourselves with compassion, kindness, humility, gentleness and patience. (Colossians 3:12)

If a person lacks patience, it is wise for them to add patience to their strengths, as Christian McCaffrey has done on the football field.

How can a person develop the virtue of patience? The answer is not profound. The only way to develop this virtue is to learn to persevere and wait! It is not something that a person can do quickly. It may be helpful to try a new hobby or volunteer work that requires some waiting and perseverance. This could involve learning to play a musical instrument, planting a garden or teaching children. Perhaps, it could involve learning a new sport. In a video game involving sports, a person can usually master the game rather quickly. However, when a person plays a real sport, it typically takes time and perseverance to excel. Ask people who have tried to master golf!

Another way to develop patience is to make a commitment to spiritual growth. Although God sometimes gives people growth spurts, spiritual growth typically occurs over a long period of time. As we spend more time with God, we come to know his immense kindness and patience. Also, as we seek to live by the Holy Spirit, we receive the fruits of the Holy Spirit, one of which is patience (Galatians 5:22).

It is good to seek God and the virtue of patience. This virtue may not come quickly or easily; but remember, God is patient.

Prayer

> God, I thank you for your immense patience. I desire to be able to respond quickly or to have patience, depending on what the situation calls for. Show me how I can develop the virtue of patience.

DEVOTION 35
WAITING FOR THE RETURN OF JESUS

On September 9, 2010, I didn't go into the church office because it was a Thursday, a day on which I usually worked at home to prepare my sermon for Sunday. I lived in a safe suburban neighborhood where people routinely walked their dogs. In the early evening, I took some food out of the refrigerator to heat up in the microwave. At that moment, my house shook slightly and I wondered what that was. When I went outside to investigate, I did not see anything wrong in front of my house, so I went back inside. However, I continued to hear some strange noises, so I went back outside again. I saw a car coming towards my house, and the driver waved at me and told me that I should leave the area. When I went back into my house and looked out through a window on the side of my house, I saw why I should leave. A huge flame that went high up into the sky appeared to be close to my house. I was terrified. I grabbed my wallet, cell phone and keys, got into my car, and drove out of the Crestmoor neighborhood in San Bruno. Later I found out that a gas pipeline had ruptured, causing a huge explosion and fire. Eight people died and many houses were destroyed or damaged. I was very fortunate. I got out safely and my house survived because it was not downwind from the fire.

What started out as a normal, peaceful day ended with a shocking, unbelievable event. This is similar to how the apostle Paul described Jesus' future return:

117

Now, brothers and sisters, about times and dates we do not need to write to you, for you know very well that the day of the Lord will come like a thief in the night. While people are saying, "Peace and safety," destruction will come on them suddenly, as labor pains on a pregnant woman, and they will not escape. But you, brothers and sisters, are not in darkness so that this day should surprise you like a thief. You are all children of the light and children of the day. We do not belong to the night or to the darkness. So then, let us not be like others, who are asleep, but let us be awake and sober. For those who sleep, sleep at night, and those who get drunk, get drunk at night. But since we belong to the day, let us be sober, putting on faith and love as a breastplate, and the hope of salvation as a helmet. (1 Thessalonians 5:1-8)

Paul used two illustrations to describe the coming of the Lord – a thief in the night and a pregnant woman having labor pains. A thief in the night is similar to the San Bruno fire, which was a totally unexpected event. Paul told the church in Thessalonica that when the Lord comes, they should not be shocked as if they were robbed by a thief in the night. Instead, they should be waiting for the Lord to return, just as a pregnant woman waits for the birth of her baby. A pregnant woman knows that the baby is coming, but doesn't know exactly when the labor pains will start. Waiting does not mean that the woman does not take any action. A wise pregnant woman prepares for the day of birth by eating healthy, avoiding alcohol and tobacco, and keeping fit. Paul exhorted the people not to be morally indifferent ("asleep")[10] but instead, to live with faith, love and hope while waiting for the return of Christ.

Many people have something that they are waiting for. Some people wait for retirement, so they can pursue something new and different in their lives. Some people wait to buy a house, especially in an expensive area. During these waiting periods, they are not passive. They prepare for the future. Similarly, God wants us to "actively wait" in response to the return of Christ. Events like the San Bruno fire remind us to be aware of Christ's imminent return and to pursue lives that are pleasing to God.

Prayer

God, I don't want to be unaware and morally indifferent when Christ returns. Although I don't know when Jesus will return, I prepare for that day. Help me to pursue a life that is pleasing to you.

DEVOTION 36
AWARENESS OF THE ENEMY

During a period of waiting, it can feel like your life is not moving forward, and you are stuck in a rut. When opportunities arise, you may pursue them and put forth your best effort, but things don't work out. Sometimes, it can even feel like your life is going backwards. Problems may arise in different areas of your life, and you may lose possessions or struggle with your health. It is natural to wonder – God, why is this happening? Am I doing something wrong or do I have a flaw or sin that I need to address? In situations like this, it is important to have discernment. It could be that you have already addressed major issues in your life and are walking with God in integrity. It could be that the enemy, Satan, is trying to bring discouragement and weaken your faith. The enemy would like nothing more than to turn people away from God.

In a time of waiting, you may experience a portion of what Job dealt with during a season of his life. Job lived with integrity and faith, and God blessed him with ten children and a multitude of livestock. Satan sought to destroy his faith by taking away his children and his possessions. God allowed Satan to do this but told Satan that he could not touch Job. When Job lost his children and possessions through different disasters and attacks by foreigners, Job mourned the losses but did not turn away from his faith in God. However, Satan did not relent:

Then the Lord said to Satan, "Have you considered my servant Job? There is no one on earth like him; he is blameless and upright, a man who fears God and shuns evil. And he still maintains his integrity, though you incited me against him to ruin him without any reason."

"Skin for skin!" Satan replied. "A man will give all he has for his own life. But now stretch out your hand and strike his flesh and bones, and he will surely curse you to your face."

The Lord said to Satan, "Very well, then, he is in your hands; but you must spare his life."

So Satan went out from the presence of the Lord and afflicted Job with painful sores from the soles of his feet to the crown of his head. Then Job took a piece of broken pottery and scraped himself with it as he sat among the ashes.

His wife said to him, "Are you still maintaining your integrity? Curse God and die!"

He replied, "You are talking like a foolish woman. Shall we accept good from God, and not trouble?"

In all this, Job did not sin in what he said. (Job 2:3-10)

After this, Job entered a difficult period of waiting for healing. Job realized that he was not perfect, but could not understand the harshness of his affliction. After all, he had led a godly, upright life. During this time, Job had three friends that came to give him counsel. Their wisdom was based on their belief that God rewarded the righteous and punished the sinner. Although their belief system had some validity, it was too simplistic and did not take into account Satan's role in what had happened to Job. Therefore, they incorrectly concluded that Job suffered as a result of his sin. They gave poor counsel to Job, who had to defend himself against the condemning words of his well-meaning friends.

One of Satan's nastiest schemes is to cause some problem in a person's life, and then get the person to falsely believe that the problem was the consequence of their own actions. This scheme can cause the person to fall into self-condemnation, which pulls the person away from God. Therefore, it is important that we have awareness of the schemes of the enemy, who tries to destroy our faith and condemn us. More importantly, we need to remember that God has authority over the enemy, and that "there is now no condemnation for those who are in Christ Jesus" (Romans 8:1) because of Jesus' shed blood for our sins.

Prayer

> God, during times that I am struggling in my life, I pray that I can hear your voice and have good discernment. If there is a sin that I need to confess and repent of, I choose to do that, knowing that "there is now no condemnation for those who are in Christ Jesus." Help me not to listen to the enemy's voice and fall into self-condemnation. Thank you that you have power and authority over the enemy.

DEVOTION 37
HUMILITY AND A DEEPER FAITH

In the previous devotional, we saw that when Job went through a period of deep pain, his three friends told him that some sin in his life was the cause of his suffering. Job held firm and stated his desire to present his case to God (Job 31:35-37). His attitude was something like this – "I want to talk to God. I am innocent and don't deserve this suffering. God needs to give me an answer for what has happened." It is not difficult to have compassion for Job, who had lost his children, possessions and health. It seems unfair that a good person like Job would suffer so much. We might wonder, "Why did God allow Satan to do some much harm to Job?"

Then, a wise person named Elihu entered the scene and began to speak to Job. Elihu felt compelled to speak because he believed that Job's friends wrongly condemned him and that Job justified himself rather than God. He spoke the following to Job:

> But those who suffer he (God) delivers in their suffering; he speaks to them in their affliction. He is wooing you from the jaws of distress to a spacious place free from restriction, to the comfort of your table laden with choice food.
>
> God is exalted in his power. Who is a teacher like him? Who has prescribed his ways for him, or said to him, 'You have done wrong'? Remember to extol his work, which people have praised in song. All humanity has seen it; mortals gaze on it from afar. How great is God—beyond our

understanding! The number of his years is past finding out. (Job 36:15-16, 22-26)

Elihu pointed out that God speaks to people in their broken-ness. Pain and suffering can open up a deeper place in a person's soul for God to reveal his majesty and glory. Elihu reminded Job of God's greatness and encouraged him to approach God with humility. Perhaps it had been difficult for Job to let down his guard and be humble before God because his three friends had pointed their fingers at him.

After Elihu gave godly wisdom to Job, God ended his silence and spoke to Job. God first gave Job this rebuke:

Who is this that obscures my plans with words without knowledge? (Job 38:2)

God proceeded with a long speech to Job, who was humbled when he gained deeper insight about God:

Then Job replied to the Lord: "I know that you can do all things; no purpose of yours can be thwarted. You asked, 'Who is this that obscures my plans without knowledge?' Surely I spoke of things I did not understand, things too wonderful for me to know. "You said, 'Listen now, and I will speak; I will question you, and you shall answer me.' My ears had heard of you but now my eyes have seen you. Therefore I despise myself and repent in dust and ashes." (Job 42:1-6)

God restored Job's health and blessed him in the latter part of his life more than in the earlier part. God gave him ten children and double the amount of livestock than what he had before.

Although Satan caused Job incredible suffering in an attempt to destroy his faith, God used this season of difficulty to do a greater work in Job and to strengthen his faith. Job emerged from this difficult season not only with his integrity, but also with humility and a deeper knowledge of God. If you are going through a season of suffering and waiting, go humbly to God in your brokenness and need. God can do a great work in your soul and bring you to a deeper faith.

Prayer

God, there may be times that my suffering seems to be unfair. In those times, help me not to focus on justifying myself and complaining about injustice. I pray that you would speak truth and bring me comfort when I am broken. I humbly surrender to you and believe that you are a great and mighty God.

DEVOTION 38
WAITING MAY BE GOD'S DISCIPLINE

The letter to the Hebrews was written to people who had gone through some difficult times. These Christians had suffered from public insult, persecution and the confiscation of their property. The author of the letter provided encouragement by giving them an explanation for their experiences:

> Endure hardship as discipline; God is treating you as his children. For what children are not disciplined by their father? If you are not disciplined—and everyone undergoes discipline—then you are not legitimate, not true sons and daughters at all. Moreover, we have all had human fathers who disciplined us and we respected them for it. How much more should we submit to the Father of spirits and live! They disciplined us for a little while as they thought best; but God disciplines us for our good, in order that we may share in his holiness. No discipline seems pleasant at the time, but painful. Later on, however, it produces a harvest of righteousness and peace for those who have been trained by it. (Hebrews 12:7-11)

The author believed that God had allowed them to go through suffering for a good purpose. God used the suffering as a form of discipline in order to build godly character in his children.

The author compared God's discipline to that of a human father, who trains his children for their good. Although a father may not like to discipline, he does it so that his children may grow up to be responsible, mature and healthy people. Part of the discipline involves teaching children to wait. Since children tend to want desirable things right away, a father may have to teach his children to:

- Wait to eat dessert until the end of the meal.

- Wait to watch TV or play video games until the homework is done.

- Wait to get a present until Christmas or their birthday.

Similarly, a season of waiting on God may be a form of discipline from God. Charles Stanley provides this insight into God's purposes for waiting:

> ...one of the most important reasons God allows us to experience seasons of waiting is to sift our motives. Why is it that we feel such distress when we are denied our heart's desire? Is it because we love it more than the Father? Are we somehow avoiding obedience or seeking to replace Him with something or someone else? Is there some sin the Lord is seeking to purge from our lives before He answers our prayers?

> Your request may be well within God's will for you, but if your motives are wrong or your tactics are sinful, He will work to align your heart with His purposes. This is not to punish you; rather, this is for your good – so that you can experience the greater freedom, more meaningful success, and deeper joy that are found only in Him. [22]

Although waiting is typically painful, it is important to remember that God is a good Father and that the discipline is for our good. In the short term, there may be pain and discouragement, but in the long term, the discipline produces a "harvest of righteousness and peace."

Prayer

God, give me the discernment to know if a season of waiting is a form of discipline. Although discipline is painful, I choose not to rebel against it. I desire that you shape me so that I can share in your holiness and experience a harvest of righteousness and peace.

DEVOTION 39
ARE YOU LIVING IN ALIGNMENT WITH YOUR VALUES?

In his book *Christian Coaching*, Gary Collins addresses a very important issue for people—living in alignment with their values. He writes:

> I have a few friends whose lives revolve around getting ahead, making money, being successful, pleasing the boss, and getting promoted. Some are committed to building a church or improving their skill in some hobby. Ask about their values and they would say that building their marriages and family are important values. They genuinely want this. They also want to be growing spiritually. But look at their lives and their habits and you see something different. Their lived-out values and their stated values are not the same. [23]

Some people may start out with a set of values but then begin to drift; perhaps getting caught up in the rat race, the demands of a fast-paced life, or just trying to keep up with the cost of living in an expensive area. Living in alignment with one's values is especially important for people who work in Silicon Valley because the area has its own particular set of values. Some of these include:

- Wealth. People may jump from company to company looking to get rich. Often, there is not much loyalty to a particular company.

- Innovation and Technology. Technology is king and people with technical skills are highly valued.

- Youth. There is a certain degree of ageism in Silicon Valley – certain companies value young people more than older people.

- Speed. The rush to get the next new hot product to market often causes people to work long hours.

God calls some people to work in high-tech, and he wants them to keep and live by his values despite the challenging environment. These words from the book of James are very relevant to high-tech workers:

> Do not merely listen to the word, and so deceive yourselves. Do what it says. Anyone who listens to the word but does not do what it says is like someone who looks at his face in a mirror and, after looking at himself, goes away and immediately forgets what he looks like. But whoever looks intently into the perfect law that gives freedom, and continues in it—not forgetting what they have heard, but doing it—they will be blessed in what they do. Those who consider themselves religious and yet do not keep a tight rein on their tongues deceive themselves, and their religion is worthless. Religion that God our Father accepts as pure and faultless is this: to look after orphans and widows in their distress and to keep oneself from being polluted by the world. (James 1:22-27)

James encouraged people to be doers of the word, not just hearers of it. He exhorted people not to have their values be "polluted by the world," but instead to live in alignment with Biblical values.

This is easier said than done. People can be drawn into making small compromises and over time, these small compromises pull them from their values. Self-deception causes them to think that they are doing fine spiritually. Someone might think, "I'm committed to God and I go to church most of the time on Sundays. I just need to get this promotion or finish this project, and then I'll spend less time at work." In reality, they may not be living in alignment with their stated values. It is important to do a periodic reality check to ensure that self-deception doesn't become a problem.

James wrote that God's word gives freedom and that doers of his word are blessed. The benefits of living in alignment with one's values include:

- Being more focused and less scattered

- Having greater inner peace

- Having better balance in one's life

- Being able to be a good example to others

Prayer

God, I choose to take time to soberly evaluate the priorities in my life. Help me not to fall into self-deception. I want to line up my life with your values. If I need to make some changes in my life, give me the courage and the wisdom to do so.

DEVOTION 40
WAITING FOR GOD'S WORD

In the workplace, some of the most challenging situations arise not because of the actual work, but because of office politics and difficult people. People sometimes act in the interest of themselves, their allies or department, and make unjust decisions that don't benefit the company as a whole. In addition, people at rival companies sometimes act ruthlessly to gain an advantage. It is easy to become disheartened and complain about unjust work situations. When we face difficult situations, we can gain wisdom from the Old Testament prophet Habakkuk, who saw ungodly behavior in both the people of his country and a foreign country.

Habakkuk saw great injustice in his country, Judah, and didn't understand why God didn't do anything about it. Habakkuk brought his complaints to God, who said that he would use the Babylonians, who were much more unrighteous than the people in Judah, to teach them a lesson. Habakkuk didn't like God's answer, so he complained again and listened for God's response:

> I will stand at my watch and station myself on the ramparts; I will look to see what he will say to me, and what answer I am to give to this complaint.

> Then the Lord replied: "Write down the revelation and make it plain on tablets so that a herald may run with it. For the revelation awaits an appointed time; it speaks of the end and will not prove false. Though it linger, wait for it; it will certainly come and will not delay. (Habakkuk 2:1-3)

Then, God told Habakkuk that in the future, he would bring an end to the rule of the Babylonians and their ungodly practices.

This passage illustrates two aspects of waiting for God's word. First, Habakkuk positioned himself to hear from God. Before taking action or speaking publicly about the situation, Habakkuk brought his complaints to God and waited to hear God's response. We can position ourselves to hear God speaking to us by engaging in spiritual practices – reading the Bible, worship, prayer and fasting. In addition, it may be helpful to have a conversation with a spiritual mentor or godly friend who can listen to complaints and help us to hear what God may be speaking to us in a particular situation.

Second, God instructed Habakkuk to write down the revelation and wait for it to be fulfilled. God said that he would deal with the Babylonians, and he was true to his word. It took quite a long time, but God raised up the Medo-Persians, who ended the rule of the Babylonians. Sometimes, God will call us to take action. At other times, he will say that he will deal with a problem or situation, so we can leave it in his hands. In such cases, taking action will inevitably lead to a much messier situation, so it is best to let God deal with it.

Waiting for God's word can not only save us from a lot of grief but also give us peace and rest. It is good to put these words into practice:

I wait for the Lord, my whole being waits, and in his word I put my hope. I wait for the Lord more than watchmen wait for the morning, more than watchmen wait for the morning. (Psalm 130:5-6)

Prayer

God, when I face frustrating situations, I pray that you would give me self-control. I choose to seek to hear your word before I take action or speak out. I desire to hear your voice. Thank you that I can trust your word.

DEVOTION 41

WAITING FOR A SPOUSE: LET GOD DIRECT YOUR STEPS

When I reached my late 30s, I felt that I had already waited a really long time for a spouse. By this point in my life, I had worked through some personal issues and felt that I was ready to be a good marriage partner. However, I had difficulty meeting the right woman, so I decided to be more proactive. I tried a Christian dating service and later enrolled in online dating. As part of the search process, I spent time thinking about what kind of woman who would be a good marriage partner for me. I don't remember everything on my list, but I recall that I wanted to find a woman who:

- Is a Christian.
- Has a compassionate heart.
- Is more outgoing than me.
- Enjoys sports.
- Is not an overseas-born Asian.

Although my ancestors are Asian, my parents and I were born in the United States. As a result, I am more "Americanized" and thought that I would fit better with someone who didn't come from a traditional Asian background.

During that period of time, I met some nice women but didn't feel that any of them were the right one. I had a humorous experience when I met a woman through online dating who went to the same church I attended! Time went by and I remained single. I became a pastor and ministered to a congregation which included married people, many of whom had children. I dated different women, but to my dismay, nothing worked out. I became very frustrated and wondered if God wanted me to be single for the rest of my life.

In 2010, I attended a Christian retreat and asked one of the prayer ministers to pray for me for a wife. Also, during that weekend, I met a friend who used to attend a small group that I led. After our meeting, my friend prayed and had a strong impression from God that she should try to set me up with her children's music teacher. My friend had a conversation with the music teacher and then contacted me to ask if I wanted to meet her.

After I exchanged some emails with the music teacher, who was named Jill, we decided to go to a restaurant for a face-to-face meeting. Originally, we didn't see each other as an ideal marriage partner. Jill was born in Taiwan, and she did not move to the United States until she went to graduate school. Also, I found out that she does not like sports at all. Jill had some reservations about meeting me because she had never thought that she would marry a pastor.

However, as we dated and got to know each other better, we found that we had good chemistry. Although Jill did not meet everything on my wish list, I found that she had many great qualities. Jill is a Christian with a compassionate heart. She is quite cute and like myself, had waited a long time to be married. I also found out that in some ways, she does not think like a traditional Asian person.

About seven months after we met, I proposed to Jill and she accepted. We were married on August 20, 2011 and as I write this, we are celebrating our 4th anniversary. Because we had been single for so long, we appreciate the wonderful blessing of marriage that God gave us. We also feel that it was worth waiting for God's timing.

I'm reminded of a passage from the book of Proverbs: "In their hearts humans plan their course, but the Lord establishes their steps." (Proverbs 16:9). I think that God would say, "You can make plans, but be open to me guiding you in a different direction."

Prayer

> Father, I praise you because you have a plan for my life and know what is best for me. Help me to be open to your leading in my life and to be patient. I choose to wait for what you think is best for my life.

DEVOTION 42
WHAT IS JESUS WAITING FOR?

Some people are surprised that I made a career change from high-tech to pastoral ministry. Although serving in full-time ministry is quite different from working in high-tech, I have found one similarity about working in these two fields—situations arise that appear to require immediate attention.

One day, Jesus faced one of these situations when he received news about a sick friend. He had an unusual response – he waited for two days before going to visit the person. If a pastor didn't go to care for a critically sick person right away, some people would likely accuse the pastor of not being a caring person. If you had been with Jesus that day, you might have asked, "What is Jesus waiting for?"

> Now a man named Lazarus was sick. He was from Bethany, the village of Mary and her sister Martha. (This Mary, whose brother Lazarus now lay sick, was the same one who poured perfume on the Lord and wiped his feet with her hair.) So the sisters sent word to Jesus, "Lord, the one you love is sick." When he heard this, Jesus said, "This sickness will not end in death. No, it is for God's glory so that God's Son may be glorified through it." Now Jesus loved Martha and her sister and Lazarus. So when he heard that Lazarus was sick, he stayed where he was two more days... (John 11:1-6)

By the time Jesus arrived in Bethany, Lazarus' body had been laid to rest in a tomb for four days. Both Martha and Mary said to Jesus, "If you had been here, my brother would not have died." (John 11:21, 11:32).

The two sisters and their friends grieved and mourned in a manner which caused Jesus to feel deeply troubled and to weep.

All of this could have been avoided if Jesus had healed Lazarus of his sickness. He had previously healed people with sicknesses from a distance and could have done so with Lazarus. However, Jesus waited because God had a different plan for this situation. After Jesus arrived in Bethany, he performed his greatest miracle by raising Lazarus from the dead. This act not only caused many people to believe in Jesus but also brought glory to God. Jesus waited to attend to this urgent matter so that God would be glorified.

You may be faced with situations in which you feel the need to take immediate action, or perhaps, God has given you an idea for doing something at work or in your ministry, and you want to implement the idea. If you are a capable person, you may want to spring into action. It's possible that God wants you to take immediate action. However, it's also possible that God wants you to wait and do things according to his timing. Sometimes, people will overreact to certain situations and take action that turns out to be unproductive or unnecessary.

We can accomplish many things through human effort, but God can accomplish more when we do things according to his timing. It is better to wait for God's timing and allow God to work in the situation even though others may not understand why you are slow to respond. Taking action in God's timing brings glory to God.

Prayer

God, I pray for your peace as I face challenging and urgent situations in my life. I choose to abide in your presence. Help me not to become stressed by events that seem to demand my immediate response. I pray that you would show me your wisdom and timing as I make decisions. I desire that my actions will bring glory to you.

DEVOTION 43
A SATISFYING JOB IS A GIFT FROM GOD

On September 6, 2015, the San Francisco Chronicle published a front page article which highlighted a major concern for high-tech entrepreneurs – mental health. The story referenced a recent study of 242 entrepreneurs which revealed that nearly half of them suffered from one or more mental health condition (depression, substance abuse, bipolar disorder and ADHD). Entrepreneurs often work in an extremely competitive and stressful environment and feel pressure to appear that they have it all together. The article reported, "In the startup community, there is little support, and a lot of fear that showing any kind of weakness will hurt morale or scare off investors." [24]

Entrepreneurs can benefit from the wisdom in the book of Ecclesiastes, which according to rabbinic tradition, was written by one of the wisest men of his times, King Solomon. Although the author had accomplished great things in his life and accumulated a tremendous amount of knowledge and wealth, he found that these things did not bring true happiness:

> What do people get for all the toil and anxious striving with which they labor under the sun? All their days their work is grief and pain; even at night their minds do not rest. This too is meaningless. A person can do nothing better than to eat and drink and find satisfaction in their own toil. This too, I see, is from the hand of God, for without him, who can eat or find enjoyment? (Ecclesiastes 2:22-25)

These words, written over 2000 years ago, have great relevance to the high-tech society today. The editors of the NIV Study Bible wrote this profound summary of the author's thinking:

> As the author looks about at the human enterprise, he sees man in mad pursuit of one thing and then another – laboring as if he could master the world, lay bare its secrets, change its fundamental structures, break through the bounds of human limitations and master his own destiny. He sees man vainly pursuing hopes and expectations that in reality are "meaningless, a chasing after the wind." [25]

The author found one of the keys to experiencing happiness – recognizing that satisfying work is a gift from God. Although God wants to give each worker the gift of a satisfying job, many people are unable to see and receive this gift.

This often occurs because people are looking for something else in their work – perhaps an opportunity to generate wealth or to be a great innovator. The result of this can be spiritual blindness, a loss of spiritual eyesight needed to see and discern God's purpose and calling for one's work. Even though high-tech entrepreneurs and workers may be brilliant and fast-thinking, they may experience dissatisfaction and problems if they cannot recognize and receive God's gift of a job that brings true satisfaction.

What would God's gift of a satisfying job look like? I believe that the job would have most or all of the following characteristics:

- The type of work interests the person and makes use of their talents and gifts.
- The workplace environment and co-workers are a good fit.

- The wages and benefits provide for the needs of the person and their family.

- The workload allows the person to have a balanced life.

- The work provides an appropriate level of challenge and the potential for growth.

- The work aligns with the person's God-given calling.

If you experience dissatisfaction or problems because of your work, seek God and ask that you can find and receive the gift of a satisfying job. The gift may be somewhat hidden and you may have to look deeply into your life and soul to find it. Some people like me have found it helpful to get assistance from a counselor, career coach or life coach in order to uncover this hidden gift. Although it may not be easy to find the gift of a satisfying job, it is a worthwhile pursuit.

Prayer

> God, I recognize that it is healthy to set limits in regards to my work. Help me to find an appropriate work-life balance. I thank you that you have the gift of a satisfying job for me. Guide and lead me to the job that you have for me.

DEVOTION 44
WAITING TO BECOME A PARENT

In the Old Testament, when men sometimes had multiple wives, a man named Elkanah married two women, Peninnah and Hannah. Peninnah bore him many children, but Hannah was barren. However, Elkanah still loved Hannah:

> Year after year this man went up from his town to worship and sacrifice to the Lord Almighty at Shiloh, where Hophni and Phinehas, the two sons of Eli, were priests of the Lord. Whenever the day came for Elkanah to sacrifice, he would give portions of the meat to his wife Peninnah and to all her sons and daughters. But to Hannah he gave a double portion because he loved her, and the Lord had closed her womb. Because the Lord had closed Hannah's womb, her rival kept provoking her in order to irritate her. This went on year after year. Whenever Hannah went up to the house of the Lord, her rival provoked her till she wept and would not eat. Her husband Elkanah would say to her, "Hannah, why are you weeping? Why don't you eat? Why are you downhearted? Don't I mean more to you than ten sons?"

> Once when they had finished eating and drinking in Shiloh, Hannah stood up. Now Eli the priest was sitting on his chair by the doorpost of the Lord's house. In her deep anguish Hannah prayed to the Lord, weeping bitterly. And she made a vow, saying, "Lord Almighty, if you will only look on your

servant's misery and remember me, and not forget your servant but give her a son, then I will give him to the Lord for
all the days of his life, and no razor will ever be used on his
head." (1 Samuel 1:3-11)

This story illustrates the problem of polygamy, which God
allowed but never intended for marriage relationships. Peninnah
subjected Hannah to a lot of "trash talking" in regards to her bar-
renness. In her distress, Hannah cried out to God and made a big sac-
rifice—if God allowed her to have a son, she would give her son to
serve the Lord. This was exactly what happened. Hannah gave birth
to Samuel and after a few years, brought her young son to live with Eli,
who trained him to become a prophet of the Lord. Samuel became
one of Israel's greatest prophets who stood strong for God. Later,
Hannah had five more children, but her first one was truly special.

People who want to become parents and struggle to conceive a
child can likely identify with the feelings that Hannah had before
she became pregnant with Samuel. Her desire to have a child became
so strong that she really couldn't take it anymore. In her desperate
state, she actually did something very wise. She expressed her feelings to the Lord and surrendered her desire to have her own child to
nurture and raise. The meaning of her vow was clear—if she had a
son, he would not be for her own well-being. Instead, her son would
live for God's glory.

The lesson from Hannah's story is not that a childless person
needs to give their firstborn to the Lord to be a prophet, missionary
or pastor in order to have a child. Hannah's story encourages us to
surrender our dreams and desires to the Lord and to make a commitment that any child bearing will be for God's glory. If a person does
this, they are in a good position to receive a special blessing from God.

Prayer

> Father, if I am waiting to become a parent, I surrender my dreams and desires to you. I thank you that you understand my pain and frustration. If you give me the gift of a child, I commit to raising the child for your glory.

DEVOTION 45
WAITING FOR GOD'S JUSTICE

One of the most difficult types of waiting occurs when a person is thrown into unfavorable and difficult circumstances because of the wrongful actions of others. Perhaps the person was seen as a threat or got in the way of someone's unethical plans and as a result, was mistreated and suffered some kind of loss. In the Old Testament, David knew this type of situation well. God had chosen David to be the future king, and David provided faithful service to the king in power, Saul. However, Saul began to be unstable due to an evil spirit and his own insecurities. Saul became jealous of David and tried to kill him. While Saul lived in a luxurious palace, David lived for many years either on the run from Saul or in exile. David survived these extremely difficult circumstances and as an old man, wrote Psalm 37, which provides guidance for such situations:

> Be still before the Lord
>   and wait patiently for him;
> do not fret when people succeed in their ways,
>   when they carry out their wicked schemes.
> Refrain from anger and turn from wrath;
>   do not fret—it leads only to evil.
> For those who are evil will be destroyed,
>   but those who hope in the Lord will inherit the land. (Psalm 37:7-9)

David pointed out two common things to avoid in these situations – anger and fretting:

- Anger – When a wrong has been committed, it is human to feel angry and want justice. It is easy to stew over what happened in the past and continue to relive the injustice and anger. Although it is normal to feel anger immediately after the hurtful event, it is important to begin the process of forgiveness and to let go.

- Fretting – This is a state of agitated worrying. A fretting person thinks, "They're going to get away with it, and I'm going to be stuck in this horrible situation." It is important for the fretting person to trust that God will bring justice and move them into a better situation.

David's counsel is to be still before God and wait patiently for him. This involves listening for God's direction and waiting for him to act. God will deal with unethical people according to his wisdom and bring justice to the situation in his timing.

When Saul hunted David and tried to eliminate him, David had two different opportunities to kill Saul, but he refrained. David knew from his relationship with God that he should not kill the Lord's anointed king. David continued to wait on God. Later, in a battle, the Philistines badly wounded Saul, who then decided to take his own life before his enemies could kill him. Seven and a half years after the death of Saul, God brought David into his destiny as the king of Israel. During those difficult years of living on the run and in exile, David developed an amazing, trusting relationship with God. In his pain and uncertainty, he sought God and learned to put his trust and hope in God, who brought about justice and his plan for David's life.

Prayer

God, I choose to forgive those who have wronged me in the past. I recognize that although they may have put me in unfavorable circumstances, they have no power to determine my destiny. Help me not to worry and to continue to be angry. Thank you that you are a God of justice and that you are in control of my destiny.

DEVOTION 46
THE VIRTUE OF SIMPLICITY

In his book *Spiritual Simplicity*, Pastor Chip Ingram writes about the Silicon Valley Shuffle, a dance step with four moves – bigger, better, faster and more. He writes,

> Our attempts to "be it all," "do it all," and "have it all" have created a complex world that:
>
> 1. Moves too fast
> 2. Delivers too little
> 3. Demands too much
>
> We don't actually say we have to be it all, do it all, and have it all, of course. We may not even be conscious that we're chasing after these things. But our actions certainly reflect that pulsating drive. And when we do this dance – intentionally or not – we create a very complex world for ourselves. [26]

Life was much simpler when I was growing up than it is for today's younger generation. To gain entrance into a good college, teenagers have to work so hard to pack their college applications with achievements in their school work, entrance exams and extracurricular activities. In 2015, Katie Couric produced a special report on Yahoo News which detailed the prevalence of mental illness on college campuses. Many young people struggle with anxiety and depression, and colleges are challenged to come up with the resources to help these students. I wonder if this problem has occurred in part because of the complexity of our culture.

How do we respond to this complexity? Many years ago, John, one of Jesus' disciples, gave this exhortation:

> Do not love the world or anything in the world. If anyone loves the world, love for the Father is not in them. For everything in the world—the lust of the flesh, the lust of the eyes, and the pride of life—comes not from the Father but from the world. The world and its desires pass away, but whoever does the will of God lives forever. (1 John 2:15-17)

John's statement about not loving the world is a little difficult to understand because he also wrote one of the most famous verses of the Bible in which Jesus said: "God so loved the world..." (John 3:16). When John wrote, "Do not love the world," I believe that he was exhorting believers not to embrace and live by the values and practices of people in the world who do not know and follow God.

How do we not love the rapid dance moves of the Silicon Valley Shuffle – bigger, better, faster and more – and instead, adopt a slower rhythm in our lives? When Jesus was asked, "Of all the commandments, which is the most important?" (Mark 12:28), he responded:

> Hear, O Israel: The Lord our God, the Lord is one. Love the Lord your God with all your heart and with all your soul and with all your mind and with all your strength.' The second is this: 'Love your neighbor as yourself.' There is no commandment greater than these. (Mark 12:29-31)

Simplifying our lives comes down to focusing our attention on loving God and loving people. Chip Ingram believes that the key to simplifying life is making love your number one priority. It takes wisdom and intentional actions to put this into practice, but it is worth the effort. In his book *Freedom of Simplicity*, Richard Foster comes to this conclusion:

> In the final analysis we are not the ones who have to untangle all the intricacies of our complex world. There are not many things we have to keep in mind – in fact, only one: to be attentive to the voice of the true Shepherd. There are not too many decisions we have to make – in fact, only one: to seek his Kingdom and his righteousness. There are not many tasks we have to do – in fact, only one: to obey him in all things. [27]

If we do these things, then we are truly loving God.

Prayer

God, although our culture pushes us to want bigger, better, faster and more, I choose to be counter-cultural and to have a simpler life. I want to place my focus on loving you and loving others. Show me how to have a simpler life and to truly love you.

DEVOTION 47
BEING THANKFUL FOR THE WAIT

Shortly before Thanksgiving Day in 2015, I considered what I was thankful for. 2015 had been somewhat of a difficult year for me. A part-time ministry position did not turn into a full-time position. Another promising potential ministry position did not work out. As Thanksgiving approached, I did not have a job and had been without full time employment for three and a half years. My thoughts turned to the waiting period that I was going through. Could I say thank you to God for the wait? I tended to look at the wait as something undesirable that I had to endure and persevere through.

I read some verses from the Bible about thankfulness. In one passage I found, the apostle Paul wrote this:

> Be very careful, then, how you live—not as unwise but as wise, making the most of every opportunity, because the days are evil. Therefore do not be foolish, but understand what the Lord's will is. Do not get drunk on wine, which leads to debauchery. Instead, be filled with the Spirit, speaking to one another with psalms, hymns, and songs from the Spirit. Sing and make music from your heart to the Lord, always giving thanks to God the Father for everything, in the name of our Lord Jesus Christ. (Ephesians 5:15-20)

The phrase "giving thanks to God the Father for everything" caught my attention. Are we really supposed to be thankful for everything that happens – including things like terrorist attacks?

The prominent Christian writer, John Stott, believed that we should not take the 'everything' in this passage too literally:

> ...the 'everything' for which we are to give thanks to God must be qualified by its context, namely in the name or our Lord Jesus Christ to God the Father. Our thanksgiving is to be for everything which is consistent with the loving Fatherhood of God and the self-revelation he has given us in Jesus Christ. [28]

After I considered this passage, I determined that 'everything' did include waiting. God had many prominent people in the Bible go through long waiting periods. Even though waiting is often not enjoyable, I decided that I needed to develop an attitude of thankfulness in regards to the waiting.

The passage also showed me something about being thankful for difficulties in life that people typically don't feel grateful for. Thankfulness for difficulty and trials comes from being filled with the Holy Spirit and cooperating with the Holy Spirit. The presence of the Holy Spirit brings peace, joy and patience, and leads people towards an attitude of thanksgiving. The Holy Spirit wants to overcome the normal thinking of human beings, which makes it very difficult to be grateful for difficult things like waiting. Therefore, it is necessary for people to cooperate with the Holy Spirit in order to develop an attitude of thanksgiving.

The presence of the Holy Spirit also helps people to gain a different perspective on their difficult situations. When I look at my period of waiting from a position of thanksgiving, I see that God has blessed my wife and me with many things during the three and a half years. My wife started a piano studio that has grown to about 40 students and has provided for a large part of our financial needs. I have had time to support my wife in her new endeavor and to spend time with her. Also, the waiting period has given me an opportunity to develop my gift of writing and to publish my first book in 2013. Last, God has taught me a lot of things during this waiting period which have made the writing of this book possible. So I thank God for the wait!

Prayer

God, I pray that you will fill me with the Holy Spirit, and that I will cooperate with your leading. Even though I have difficulties in my life, I praise you and thank you because through these challenges, you are shaping me and molding me into the person you want me to be. I thank you that you are a good and loving Father.

DEVOTION 48
WAITING FOR HEALING

In the gospel accounts of Jesus's ministry, one recurring theme is his healing of sick people. Sometimes, as in the following story, people went through a long period of suffering and illness before they experienced healing:

A large crowd followed and pressed around him (Jesus). And a woman was there who had been subject to bleeding for twelve years. She had suffered a great deal under the care of many doctors and had spent all she had, yet instead of getting better she grew worse. When she heard about Jesus, she came up behind him in the crowd and touched his cloak, because she thought, "If I just touch his clothes, I will be healed." Immediately her bleeding stopped and she felt in her body that she was freed from her suffering.

At once Jesus realized that power had gone out from him. He turned around in the crowd and asked, "Who touched my clothes?" "You see the people crowding against you," his disciples answered, "and yet you can ask, 'Who touched me?'" But Jesus kept looking around to see who had done it. Then the woman, knowing what had happened to her, came and fell at his feet and, trembling with fear, told him the whole truth. He said to her, "Daughter, your faith has healed you. Go in peace and be freed from your suffering." (Mark 5:24-34)

Jesus made an interesting statement – "your faith has healed you." What did Jesus mean when he said this? Faith is about who and what you put your trust in. It appears that for many years, the woman had believed in her doctors and their medical knowledge because she spent all her money on them. Although this may have been the logical course of action to take, it did not work. Ultimately, after this long ordeal, she believed that Jesus had the power to heal her, put her faith in him and sought him out. As a result, she was healed.

When this healing occurred almost 2000 years ago, the doctors had very limited medical knowledge. Since then, amazing advances in medical research and technology have occurred. The Biotechnology industry has grown significantly, especially in the geographic areas close to Silicon Valley. Although our society has benefited tremendously from all the progress in medical research and practice, people can still suffer from health problems that doctor struggle to resolve. I recently received a holiday letter from a friend who reported that a family member's illness had lasted for months, and that doctors had not been able to diagnose the problem correctly.

God can use medical technology and doctors to bring healing to people but sometimes, even modern medical practices are not enough. Situations arise that require the touch of God's healing power. Over the last two decades, I have participated on prayer ministry teams and I have been amazed to see God heal people. It is difficult to understand exactly how God's healing power works. In some cases, the healing happens instantaneously. In other cases, the sick person has to wait and the healing happens over a period of time. Sometimes, healing does not occur. The apostle Paul suffered from what he described as a "thorn in my flesh" and pleaded with God to take it away. The Lord did not remove it and told him, "My grace is sufficient for you, for my power is made perfect in weakness." (2 Cor. 12:8).

If you need healing, it is good to learn about your condition, and seek medical advice and treatment. However, it is more important to put your faith in Jesus and seek him fervently. He is the one with the power to heal.

Prayer

God, I am thankful for all the advancements that have been made in the medical field. However, I recognize that you are the one who created me, and that you have greater knowledge than my doctors. I put my faith in you in regards to my health. If I have a physical ailment, I pray that your healing power would touch me.

DEVOTION 49
WAITING FOR A GLORIFIED BODY

With the high price of housing in Silicon Valley, some people find it beneficial to buy an older house and renovate it. My wife Jill thinks this may be a good strategy and frequently watches Home and Garden Television's *Fixer Upper*, which features the home renovation business of Chip and Joanna Gaines. This couple finds old, dilapidated homes that don't appear to have much value and renovates them for clients. At the end of each show, Chip and Joanna reveal their work to their clients, who typically are stunned and amazed by the transformation. They can hardly believe what has happened to their houses!

Unfortunately, there is no real "fixer upper" for our physical bodies here on earth. Although people may use cosmetic surgery or Viagra to appear to be youthful, there is no escape. As we get older, our bodies begin to break down. I used to play a number of different sports when I was younger—basketball, softball, volleyball—but now just play golf and tennis (doubles, not singles!). My body is not as strong and flexible, and I want to try to minimize aches, pains and injuries. The decline of physical health as we get older can be depressing.

However, there is good news. In heaven, believers in Christ will experience an incredible transformation. The apostle Paul wrote about this in the New Testament:

> Not only so, but we ourselves, who have the first fruits of the Spirit, groan inwardly as we wait eagerly for our adoption to sonship, the redemption of our bodies. For in this hope we were saved. But hope that is seen is no hope at all. Who hopes for what they already have? But if we hope for what we do not yet have, we wait for it patiently. (Romans 8:23-25)

But our citizenship is in heaven. And we eagerly await a Savior from there, the Lord Jesus Christ, who, by the power that enables him to bring everything under his control, will transform our lowly bodies so that they will be like his glorious body. (Philippians 3:20-21)

Paul points out some very good news for believers – we will get redeemed, glorious bodies in heaven! In the previous devotion, we considered that God sometimes heals people with physical ailments. In cases in which God does not heal, all hope is not lost. We can look forward to what will happen when we get to heaven. Biblical scholar N.T. Wright describes the new body we will have in heaven:

The body is intended to be glorious, splendid, fashioned after the model of Jesus' resurrected body, no longer subject to weakness, humiliation, sickness, sin, and death.[29]

This does not mean that we do not make efforts to take care of our physical bodies. Paul pointed that physical training has value in our life here on earth (1 Timothy 4:8). Maintaining good physical health through a proper exercise and diet regime helps us to serve God effectively during our lifetime. However, if you have done what you can and your body is starting to feel like a "fixer upper," don't despair too much. Jesus has a glorified body for you in heaven.

Prayer

God, thank you for the body that you have given me. I want to take care of myself so that I can serve you effectively. However, as my body deteriorates as I get older, help me not to get depressed. I look forward to the day when you will give me a glorified body in heaven.

DEVOTION 50
THINGS CAN HAPPEN LATER IN LIFE

The media has taken notice of a trend in Silicon Valley – younger people are valued more than older people. Reuters published a special report titled, "Silicon Valley's Dirty Secret – Age Bias," which stated:

> ... the youth worship undercuts another of Silicon Valley's cherished ideals: that anyone smart and driven can get ahead in what the industry likes to think of as an egalitarian culture. To many, it looks like simple age discrimination – and it's affecting people who wouldn't fit any normal definition of old. [30]

Dan Scheinman, the former head of mergers and acquisitions at Cisco Systems, noticed this trend when he looked for potential investing opportunities in start-up companies. Typically, twenty-something entrepreneurs found it easier to acquire venture capital financing than their counterparts in their 40s and 50s. Scheinman came to realize that older entrepreneurs were "the mother of all undervalued opportunities," and began to invest in start-up companies run by chief executive officers age 35 or older. One of these companies, Tango, a mobile messaging company, had a CEO who was getting close to age 50 when Scheinman invested. Respected venture capitalists told Scheinman that this CEO had no chance of success. However, Tango now has over 300 million registered members and has received funding from Alibaba, the Chinese e-commerce giant.

Even in the youthful culture of Silicon Valley, older adults can still make an impact. [31]

A man in the Bible had a great impact during the latter part of his life. Moses, who lived to be 120 years old, had the most significant years of his life between the ages of 80 and 120. During Moses' middle years (ages 40-80), he lived in a desolate area after fleeing from Egypt. Moses had this encounter with God at the age of 80:

> After forty years had passed, an angel appeared to Moses in the flames of a burning bush in the desert near Mount Sinai. When he saw this, he was amazed at the sight. As he went over to get a closer look, he heard the Lord say: "I am the God of your fathers, the God of Abraham, Isaac and Jacob.' Moses trembled with fear and did not dare to look. Then the Lord said to him, 'Take off your sandals, for the place where you are standing is holy ground. I have indeed seen the oppression of my people in Egypt. I have heard their groaning and have come down to set them free. Now come, I will send you back to Egypt." (Acts 7:30-34)

When God called Moses, he was tending the sheep that belonged to his father in-law Jethro. This job seemingly did not make the best use of Moses' talents and capabilities. Moses had been raised in the Pharaoh's household and had received the best education available in Egypt. During Moses' 40 years in the desolate area, it looked like that this education had been wasted. However, God used this time to prepare Moses to shepherd his people and to lead them out of slavery in Egypt.

Sometimes, people may have to wait until later in life to find and live out their God-given calling. God uses people of different ages to accomplish his purposes, and he doesn't want people to give in to believing what the high-tech culture thinks is valuable. No matter your age, God has a plan and purpose for your life.

Prayer

> God, help me to find my value in what you say about me, not about what the culture says. Help me to serve you faithfully in the task you have currently given me. I trust that you will bring about your plans for my life in your good timing.

DEVOTION 51
WAITING TO SEE JESUS

In 2015, the Golden State Warriors won the National Basketball Association championship by defeating LeBron James and the Cleveland Cavaliers in the NBA Finals. The Warriors were led by two Christians – Stephen Curry, who won the Most Valuable Player award for the 2014-2015 season, and Andre Iguodala, who won the Most Valuable Player award for the NBA Finals. The last time that the Warriors won the championship was in 1975, so their fans had waited 40 years (a Biblical number for waiting!) for a championship. Warrior fans had suffered through many difficult, losing seasons before celebrating the victory of an exciting and talented team.

Sports are very important for many people in America. Sometimes the media will identify an older fan who just wants to see their team win a championship before they die. In the Bible, there was a man who waited to see a very important person before he died:

> Now there was a man in Jerusalem called Simeon, who was righteous and devout. He was waiting for the consolation of Israel, and the Holy Spirit was on him. It had been revealed to him by the Holy Spirit that he would not die before he had seen the Lord's Messiah. Moved by the Spirit, he went into the temple courts. When the parents brought in the child Jesus to do for him what the custom of the Law required, Simeon took him in his arms and praised God, saying:
>
> "Sovereign Lord, as you have promised,

161

you may now dismiss your servant in peace.
For my eyes have seen your salvation,
which you have prepared in the sight of all nations:
a light for revelation to the Gentiles,
and the glory of your people Israel." (Luke 2:25-32)

Simeon had seen Israel go through many difficult years under the oppressive rule of the Roman Empire. Like other Jewish people, he waited for the appearance of the consolation of Israel, the Messiah. Many Jewish people hoped that the Messiah would remove Roman rule and restore the nation of Israel to its former glory. However, Simeon recognized that Jesus the Messiah was not just for the Jewish people; he was for people of all nations. Simeon was able to see the true person of Jesus.

When Jesus grew up and started his ministry, he spoke some words that described Simeon: "Blessed are the pure in heart, for they will see God." (Matthew 5:8). Simeon remained devoted to God until his elderly years, and God rewarded him with a great opportunity – seeing Jesus the Messiah in the flesh and holding him in his arms. Although we may go through periods of waiting and difficult times, it is important to stay devoted to the Lord. God may have a special blessing in store for you.

Prayer

God, help me to stay devoted to you even as I go through periods of difficulty and waiting. I thank you that you sent your son, Jesus, for the salvation of all people.

DEVOTION 52
AN IMPORTANT SCRIPTURE TO REMEMBER

As we conclude this series of devotions about waiting on God, we will take a look at one final Scripture that is important to remember. In the following passage, the prophet Isaiah addressed a situation in which the Israelites had turned away from God, and their nation had crumbled. Isaiah's dialogue with God contained some very important truths:

Since ancient times no one has heard, no ear has perceived, no eye has seen any God besides you, who acts on behalf of those who wait for him. You come to the help of those who gladly do right, who remember your ways. But when we continued to sin against them, you were angry. How then can we be saved?

All of us have become like one who is unclean, and all our righteous acts are like filthy rags; we all shrivel up like a leaf, and like the wind our sins sweep us away. No one calls on your name or strives to lay hold of you; for you have hidden your face from us and have given us over to our sins. Yet you, Lord, are our Father. We are the clay, you are the potter; we are all the work of your hand. (Isaiah 64:4-8)

Isaiah made a very clear statement about waiting—God takes action for people who wait for him. This is a very important truth to remember and to live by. God wants his people to wait for and trust in him. Unfortunately, this did not happen in ancient Israel during the time when Isaiah lived. All too often, the Israelites turned away from

God and worshipped foreign gods. Also, they sometimes ignored God and took matters into their own hands (see Isaiah 30).

This situation is a microcosm of humanity's tendency to be alienated from God. One consequence of this alienation is that people generally have difficulty waiting on God, so they do not benefit from God acting on their behalf. Isaiah asked a very good question: "How then can we be saved?" (Isaiah 64:5). Ultimately, the only solution is the salvation offered by Jesus Christ, who provides a way for humanity to be reconciled with God. By dying for our sins that separate us from God, Jesus allows us to have a relationship with God.

This salvation is more than just a one-time event. The apostle Paul encouraged believers to "continue to work out your salvation with fear and trembling" (Philippians 2:12). I believe that part of working out our salvation involves learning to wait on God. God uses times of waiting to mold us and shape us. The passage from Isaiah reminds us that we have a good Father who molds us like a potter who molds clay. When we feel broken or lacking during times of waiting, God can shape us into the people that He wants us to be. He can develop our characters. He can give us more faith, patience, healing, perseverance and wisdom.

Our frantic high-tech society tends to make us believe that we need to make things happen quickly. Remember, we have a God who makes good things happen for us when we wait for him. This is a very comforting truth.

Prayer

> God, I desire to remember this verse, "Since ancient times no one has heard, no ear has perceived, no eye has seen any God besides you, who acts on behalf of those who wait for him." (Isaiah 64:4). In times when I struggle during a season of waiting, I pray that you would bring this verse to my mind. I trust that you will act as I wait on you.

END NOTES

[1] Charles F. Stanley, *Waiting on God: Strength for Today and Hope for Tomorrow* (New York: Howard Books, 2015), 9.

[2] Stephanie Brown, *Speed: Facing Our Addiction to Fast and Faster – and Overcoming Our Fear of Slowing Down* (New York: Berkley, 2014), Kindle edition.

[3] Stanley, *Waiting on God*, 66.

[4] Dennis Bratcher, "Ba'al Worship in the Old Testament," *The Voice*, Christian Resource Institute. http://www.crivoice.org/baal.html. Accessed September 16, 2015.

[5] C.S. Lewis, *Mere Christianity* (San Francisco: HarperSanFrancisco, 2001), 122.

[6] Os Hillman, "Competition: A Word Not Found in the Bible," *The Christian Post*, August 21, 2013.

http://www.christianpost.com/news/
competition-a-word-not-found-in-the-bible-102747/

[7] Erika Harrell and Lynn Langton, "Victims of Identity Theft, 2012." *U.S. Department of Justice*, December 2013. http://www.bjs.gov/content/pub/pdf/vit12.pdf

[8] Sarah Young, *Jesus Calling* (Nashville: Thomas Nelson, 2004), 228.

[9] Melissa Carroll, "UH Study Links Facebook Use to Depressive Symptoms," *University of Houston*, April 6, 2015.

http://www.uh.edu/news-events/stories/2015/
April/040415FaceookStudy.php

[10] Lev Grossman, "How J.J. Abrams Brought Back Star Wars Using Puppets, Greebles and Yak Hair," *Time*, December 14, 2015.

[11] Grossman, "How J.J. Abrams Brought Back Star Wars Using Puppets, Greebles and Yak Hair."

[12] Brown, *Speed*.

[13] Brown, *Speed*.

[14] Chris Tomlin, Jesse Reeves and Martin Smith, "Waiting Here for You," sung by Christy Nockels, *WOW Worship Deluxe Edition* (Provident Music Group, 2014), compact disc.

[15] Gary R. Collins, *Christian Coaching* (Colorado Springs: NavPress, 2009), 160.

[16] Stanley, *Waiting on God*, 80-81.

[17] Brown, *Speed*.

[18] U.S. News & World Report, "Best High Schools in California," http://www.usnews.com/education/best-high-schools/california

Accessed February 26, 2016.

[19] Timothy Keller, *Counterfeit Gods: The Empty Promises of Money, Sex, and Power, and the Only Hope that Matters* (New York: Penguin, 2009), xvii.

[20] Educational Testing Service and Ad Council, "Cheating is a Personal Foul,"

http://www.glass-castle.com/clients/www-nocheating-org/adcouncil/research/cheatingfactsheet.html

Accessed February 17, 2016.

[21] Connor Letourneau, "Cal Focuses on Limiting Stanford's Christian McCaffrey," *San Francisco Chronicle*, November 17, 2015.

http://www.sfgate.com/collegesports/article/Cal-focuses-on-limiting-Stanford-s-Christian-6639483.php

[22] Stanley, *Waiting on God*, 19.

[23] Collins, *Christian Coaching*, 146.

[24] Greta Kaul, "Suicide Concerns in Tech Industry," *San Francisco Chronicle*, September 6, 2015.

[25] Kenneth Barker, ed., *The NIV Study Bible* (Grand Rapids: Zondervan Publishing House, 1995), 984.

[26] Chip Ingram, *Spiritual Simplicity: Doing Less, Loving More* (New York: Howard Books, 2013), 8.

[27] Richard J. Foster, *Freedom of Simplicity* (New York: HarperCollins, 1981), 184.

[28] John Stott, *The Message of Ephesians* (Leicester, England: IVP Academic, 1984), 207.

[29] N.T. Wright, "The Letter to the Romans," *The New Interpreter's Bible* (Nashville: Abingdon Press, 2002), 598.

[30] Sarah McBride, "Special Report: Silicon Valley's Dirty Secret – Age Bias," *Reuters*, November 27, 2012. http://www.reuters.com/article/us-valley-ageism-idUSBRE8AQ0JK20121127

[31] Noam Scheiber, "The Brutal Ageism of Tech," *New Republic*, June 19, 2014.

http://www.newrepublic.com/article/117088/silicons-valleys-brutal-ageism

BIBLIOGRAPHY

Barker, Kenneth, ed. *The NIV Study Bible*. Grand Rapids: Zondervan Publishing House, 1995.

Bratcher, Dennis. "Ba'al Worship in the Old Testament," *The Voice*, Christian Resource Institute. Accessed September 16, 2015. http://www.crivoice.org/baal.html

Brown, Stephanie. *Speed: Facing Our Addiction to Fast and Faster – and Overcoming Our Fear of Slowing Down*. New York: Berkley, 2014, Kindle edition.

Carroll, Melissa, "UH Study Links Facebook Use to Depressive Symptoms," *University of Houston*, April 6, 2015. http://www.uh.edu/news-events/stories/2015/April/040415FaceookStudy.php

Collins, Gary R. *Christian Coaching*. Colorado Springs: NavPress, 2009.

Couric, Katie, "*Students in Crisis: Mental Health & Suicide on College Campuses*," Yahoo News, Accessed May 14, 2015. https://news.yahoo.com/mental-health-suicide-on-college-campuses-katie-couric-141742009.html#sapphireChapter1

Educational Testing Service and Ad Council, "Cheating is a Personal Foul," Accessed February 17, 2016. http://www.glass-castle.

com/clients/www-nocheating-org/adcouncil/research/cheat-ingfactsheet.html

Foster, Richard J. *Freedom of Simplicity*. New York: HarperCollins, 1981.

Grossman, Lev. "How J.J. Abrams Brought Back Star Wars Using Puppets, Greebles and Yak Hair," *Time*, December 14, 2015.

Harrell, Erika and Langton, Lynn. "Victims of Identity Theft, 2012," *U.S. Department of Justice*, December 2013. http://www.bjs.gov/content/pub/pdf/vit12.pdf

Hillman, Os. "Competition: A Word Not Found in the Bible," *The Christian Post*, August 21, 2013. http://www.christianpost.com/news/competition-a-word-not-found-in-the-bible-102747/

Ingram, Chip. *Spiritual Simplicity: Doing Less, Loving More*. New York: Howard Books, 2013.

Kaul, Greta. "Suicide Concerns in Tech Industry," *San Francisco Chronicle*, September 6, 2015.

Keller, Timothy, *Counterfeit Gods: The Empty Promises of Money, Sex, and Power, and the Only Hope that Matters*, New York: Penguin, 2009.

Letourneau, Connor. "Cal Focuses on Limiting Stanford's Christian McCaffrey," *San Francisco Chronicle*, November 17, 2015. http://www.sfgate.com/collegesports/article/Cal-focuses-on-limiting-Stanford-s-Christian-6639483.php

Lewis, C.S. *Mere Christianity*. San Francisco: HarperSanFrancisco, 2001.

McBride, Sarah. "Special Report: Silicon Valley's Dirty Secret – Age Bias," *Reuters*, November 27, 2012. http://www.reuters.com/article/us-valley-ageism-idUSBRE8AQ0JK20121127

Scheiber, Noam. "The Brutal Ageism of Tech," *New Republic*, June 19, 2014. http://www.newrepublic.com/article/117088/silicons-valleys-brutal-ageism

Stanley, Charles F. *Waiting on God: Strength for Today and Hope for Tomorrow*. New York: Howard Books, 2015.

Stott, John. *The Message of Ephesians*. Leicester, England: IVP Academic, 1984.

Tomlin, Chris, Reeves, Jesse and Smith, Martin, "Waiting Here for You," sung by Christy Nockels, *WOW Worship Deluxe Edition*. Provident Music Group, 2014, compact disc.

U.S. News & World Report. "Best High Schools in California." Accessed February 26, 2016. http://www.usnews.com/education/best-high-schools/california

Williams, David. 1 and 2 Thessalonians. Peabody, MA: Hendrickson Publishers, 1995.

Wright, N.T. "The Letter to the Romans," *The New Interpreter's Bible*. Nashville: Abingdon Press, 2002.

Young, Sarah, *Jesus Calling*. Nashville: Thomas Nelson, 2004.

ABOUT THE AUTHOR

Ron is a graduate of Stanford University (BS Industrial Engineering) and UC Berkeley (MBA). During his time in high-tech, he worked for Tandem Computers and PeopleSoft. After God called Ron into full-time ministry, he graduated from Fuller Seminary with a Master's degree in Theology and served as a pastor in San Francisco for almost six years. He is the author of *A Stanford Degree Won't Get You into Heaven: Jesus' Journey to Wholeness for Asian Americans*. Ron lives with his wife Jill in Fremont, California.

If you are interested in contacting Ron about a speaking engagement, please send an email message to him at ronchin414@ yahoo.com.

CPSIA information can be obtained
at www.ICGtesting.com
Printed in the USA
FSOW02n0058060516
20114FS